MW00861536

Handbook of the Seneca Language

BY

WALLACE L. CHAFE

Temporary Scientist

Anthropological Survey

New York State Museum and Science Service

The University of the State of New York

The State Education Department

Albany, 1963

M582-Mr 62-2000 (1H2-120)
REPRINTED 2007
GLOBAL LANGUAGE PRESS
TORONTO

© 2007 Global Language Press
New covers and front matter
First published 1963 by The State Education Departmrent, Albany, New York
Reprinted 2007 by Global Language Press

Global Language Press
238-1170 Bay St
Toronto, ON M5S 2B4
CANADA
http://language-press.com

isbn: 1-897367-13-9

Printed in the United States of America

Contents

HANDBOOK OF THE SENECA LANGUAGE

By

Wallace L. Chafe*

Introduction

This work is intended as a practical guide to the Seneca language for those with no linguistic training and for those who are to some degree familiar with linguistic concepts and terminology, but to whom the field is not a specialty. Widespread interest in the Seneca Indians was stimulated during the infancy of scientific anthropology by Lewis Henry Morgan's *League of the Ho-dé-no-sau-nee or Iroquois*, originally published in 1851, and this interest continues to this day among a large group of scholars, both professional and amateur. The language is always a point of concern, and a number of people have expressed the need for a book of this nature. The author is grateful to William N. Fenton, Assistant Commissioner for the New York State Museum and Science Service, and to many individuals on the Allegany, Cattaraugus, and Tonawanda reservations in New York for their indispensable assistance. Edgar M. Reilly, Jr., and Stanley J. Smith, both of the New York State Museum, provided most of the zoological and botanical scientific names, and both the latter and Elisabeth J. Tooker made useful suggestions with regard to the text.

The book consists of three parts. Section I, on orthography, describes a way of writing Seneca words consistently and without omitting features that are significant. Various spelling systems have been used, and are being used, for the writing of Seneca by missionaries, anthropologists, and the speakers of the language themselves. Everyone has his own system, although most orthographies used by the Seneca themselves can be traced to missionary origins in the 19th century. Among anthropologists, from Morgan to Fenton, there has been practically no standardization at all. Both Morgan and Parker, two of the most prolific writers on the Seneca, were extremely poor phoneticians, and their transcriptions of Seneca words are far from satisfac-

* Bureau of American Ethnology, Smithsonian Institution, Washington 25, D. C.

1

tory. The aim of section I is to promote an accurate, consistent, and standardized way of writing Seneca terms for all who may have occasion to do so.

Section II, on grammar, is concerned with the structure of Seneca words. It is no more than an outline of a highly complex subject. Those who wish to pursue the subject further are referred to the author's more technical publication, *Seneca Morphology*.[1]

No claim is made for the completeness of section III, the glossary. It is not intended as a Seneca dictionary. The basis on which items have been included is their past occurrence or the likelihood of their future occurrence in the anthropological literature. Even today, Seneca culture is rich and many-sided, and the author cannot claim to have had contact with all its facets nor to have examined thoroughly all that has been written about it. The terminology relating to the Iroquois Confederacy may be particularly incomplete. Vocabulary peculiar to the Christian community and the Seneca Nation's government has been almost wholly neglected. It is hoped that the section on orthography will permit accurate transcription of whatever terms are not included.

[1] See Bibliography.

I. Orthography

"Almost every man who writes Indian words, spells them in a peculiar manner." (Jonathan Edwards, 1788)

This section provides the information that is needed to write individual Seneca words, and it is assumed that this will be the primary interest of the users of this book. For the writing of sentences and longer pieces of text, thoroughness would demand the marking of certain other features—for example, pitch contours and pauses—which are not introduced here. It is suggested that this section will be most valuable if it is reviewed systematically with the help of a native speaker of Seneca, who can be asked to pronounce the examples given, repeating them as often as necessary. An attempt has been made to provide forms that can be easily elicited by means of the English translations: by asking such questions as "How do you say . . . ?" The glossary provides abundant further material for practice.

Writing has as its purpose the representation of the spoken language. The system of writing used for English is notoriously lacking in consistency. On the one hand, a single spelling, like *read*, may stand for more than one pronunciation, while, on the other hand, the same pronunciation may be represented by several different spellings, as in the case of *to, too,* and *two.* Our spelling conventions are interwoven with related traditions and are not readily subject to change; one needs only to think of the millions of books now in existence. But with a language that does not have a long written history—and most of the world's languages belong in this category—one clearly should take advantage of the opportunity for consistent representation of its sounds. In the last quarter century, linguistic science has made great strides in understanding the nature of linguistic sound systems, and hence in providing the basis for satisfactory writing systems. The crucial consideration is to symbolize only and all the sound distinctions which are used in the language to distinguish meanings. For example, Seneca has a sound which seems to us to be like English *k,* and another which seems like *g.* Nowhere, however, does Seneca distinguish words of different meaning by the difference between these two sounds, a difference in "voicing"; that is, the lack or presence of vibration in the vocal chords. The *k* and *g* sounds differ only in regard to voicing, and its lack or presence is entirely determined by the surrounding sounds in a particular word. The difference between *k* and *g* is thus not distinctive, and linguists call them members of the same phoneme. The spelling system presented here utilizes one symbol for each phoneme. Thus for any spoken word there is only one possible spelling, and for any spelling there is only one possible spoken equivalent. What symbols are used is not so important as how they are used; **k** was chosen for the phoneme described above. Four symbols used here, the acute accent mark ('), the symbol **ʔ** (the top part of a question mark), and the vowel symbols **ɛ** and **ɔ** are not present on a standard typewriter. In typing they can be written in by hand, or other symbols can be substituted for them.

It is impossible to compare accurately the sounds of one language with those of another; but, since the orientation of this book precludes technical phonetic descriptions, comparison with familiar languages is the only available means of conveying an idea of the sounds discussed. Some of the sounds and symbols are more easily relatable to German than to English, and readers who have some familiarity with German may be helped by the comparisons with that language. However, nothing can substitute for listening to the Seneca words from the lips of a native speaker.

Seneca has a relatively small number of phonemes, as languages go, and its words can be written by using 16 letters plus the colon (:) and the acute accent mark. The letters used to represent the vowels are **a, ä, e, ɛ, i, o**, and **ɔ**. The consonants are represented by **h, j, k, n, s, t, w, y**, and **ʔ**.

The colon is used to represent lengthening (increased duration) of the preceding vowel; compare the length of the vowels in **wis** 'five', **kawɛ:ni:s** 'a long word', **kawɛni:sɔs** 'long words'. Between two vowels, however, it indicates a lengthening of the whole vowel sequence. Thus, **a:ɛ** has two vowels of equivalent length, but each is one and a half times as long as the vowels in **aɛ**; compare **waɛʔ** 'he said it,' **wa:ɛʔ** 'he put it in it.' It may also occur between two identical vowels; for example, **kaka:aʔ** 'story, tale,' where the **a:a** is three times as long as the first **a**.

The accent mark indicates a greater degree of loudness, usually accompanied by a relatively higher pitch, on the vowel over which it is written; compare wá:ɛʔ 'he put it on it,' kaká:ʔ 'its eye' with wa:ɛʔ, kaka:aʔ just cited.

As can be seen from the examples, not all words contain either vowel length or the accent. While a word may contain more than one long vowel, however, no word in isolation ever contains more than one accent. One other generalization that it is well to keep in mind is that no word spoken by itself (outside of a longer sentence) begins with a vowel or ends with either a vowel or n, w, or y. The reader may find difficulty in recognizing ʔ at the beginning of words that may seem to start with a vowel and in identifying ʔ and h at the ends of words. The final t and k after ɛ and ɔ may also cause trouble. These points are discussed below in connection with each phoneme.

The Vowels

The letters a, e, i, and o, with certain exceptions described below, represent approximately the same sounds as do these letters in the writing of German long vowels; for example, as in German *Hahn* 'rooster,' *zehn* 'ten,' *ihn* 'him,' and *Sohn* 'son.' The sound represented by ä is roughly like that of *a* in English *man*. Disregarding the other letters for the moment, note the sound of

a in ska:t 'one,' wahtaʔ 'maple.'
ä in ká:hkwa:ʔ sun or moon, ʔoʔkáʔthɛʔ 'I climbed'
e in ʔi:ke:t 'I'm standing,' ʔi:ke 'I'm walking, going'
i in tekhni:h 'two,' wis 'five'
o in hakso:t 'my grandfather,' ʔonóʔja 'tooth'

The vowels written a, ä, e, and o have a somewhat different sound when they are immediately followed by i, j, k, s, or t (but not with an intervening :; that is, not when they are long). In this case,

a sounds roughly like the *u* in English *hut*: note the second a in ja:tak 'seven,' the a in kyɛthwas 'I plant'
ä sounds roughly like the *e* in English *met*: note the ä in ʔoʔkhät 'I passed by,' so:wäk 'duck'
e sounds roughly like the *i* in English *hit*: note the first e in sneké:äh 'take a drink!,' the e in testas 'stand it up!'
o sounds roughly like the *u* in English *put*: note the second o in ʔo:nekanos 'water,' the o in ʔóiwaʔ 'cause, matter, word'

Two vowels have not yet been considered: the nasalized vowels written ɛ and ɔ. The former sounds something like the French nasalized vowel in *bien*, while the latter sounds roughly like the vowel of English *dawn* pronounced through the nose. Note the sound of

ɛ in washɛ:h 'ten,' sɛh 'three'
ɔ in tyohto:h 'nine,' tekyɔ? 'eight'
both vowels in kɛjɔh 'fish,' ?onɛ́ɔ? 'corn'

The vowel a is also nasalized when it occurs just before ɛ or ɔ; note its sound in waɛ? 'he said it,' káɔhta?keh 'on my ear.'

The Consonants

The letters **n, w,** and **y** represent sounds approximately the same as those which they commonly represent in English spelling. Note the sound of

n in niwá?a:h 'how small it is,' ?onónɔ?ta? 'potato'
w in wis 'five,' ?osno:we? 'it's fast, speedy'
y in ye:i? 'six,' kanyáhtɛ:h 'snapping turtle'

The combinations **sy, ty,** and **thy** are discussed separately below.

The sound represented by **s,** except in the combination **sy** and directly before a vowel, is also like that commonly associated with the same letter in English. Before a vowel, **s** has a more relaxed articulation which is apt to sound like *z* to English-speaking listeners, particularly between two vowels. Note the **s** in ska:t 'one,' washɛ:h 'ten,' kanɔ́hse:s 'longhouse,' wasa:se? 'war dance.' When the combination **ts** occurs before **i,** the tongue is closer to the palate, yielding a sound somewhat like the *ch* in English *cheer*; for example, wɛ:nítsi:yo:h 'beautiful day,' tsi?tyɔ? 'you stay there' (but see **thy** below).

The letter **k** represents a sound about like that spelled *k* in English as long as it is followed by **h, s, t,** or **?.** Otherwise—that is, before **w, y,** or a vowel (it never occurs before **n, j,** or another **k**)—**k** represents a sound like that written *g* in English *good.* Note the **k** in hakso:t 'my grandfather,' ktakhe? 'I'm running,' niwák?a:h 'how short it is,' ja:tak 'seven,' kwa?yɔ:? 'rabbit,' kyashɛ? 'I'm lying,' kekɔ́ta?keh 'on my nose.' At the end of a word after a nasalized vowel, **k** may sound as if it is preceded or even replaced by a sound like that at the end of English *song*; note hatɔ́:k 'he used to say it.'

Analogously, the letter **t** represents a sound like that of the same letter in English, when it is followed by **h, k, s,** or **?.** Otherwise, that is, before **n, w, y,** or a vowel—it occurs before **n** only in the word ʔóätnɛʔtaʔ 'fern,' never before j or another t—t represents a sound like that written d in English. Note t in ʔoʔkátkathoʔ 'I looked at it,' wɛːnítsiːyoːh 'beautiful day,' ʔoʔnótʔah (the name of the third month), skaːt 'one,' tɛtwaːt 'we'll dance,' teotitáʔɔh 'they have stood up.' At the end of a word after a nasalized vowel, t often sounds like an n that is abruptly cut off; note ʔoʔkyɛt 'I hit it,' ʔohsikwɛɔt 'rattlesnake' (note that n never occurs at the end of a word).

The letter j represents a sound similar to that written dz in the English word adze; note the j in kɛjɔh 'fish,' joʔäːkaʔ 'raccoon.' Before i the tongue is closer to the palate, yielding a sound that English-speaking listeners may be apt to interpret as the sound represented by j in English jeer (but see ty below); note the j in kajiːstaʔ 'light, glow, ember,' jiːyäh 'dog.'

The sound written h is quite similar to the sound written with that letter in English, but occurs in positions where it does not occur in English: notably after a vowel, at the end of a word, and before n. Note h in hataːkheʔ 'he's running,' kahókaːɛt 'doorway,' wahtaʔ 'maple,' sɛh 'three,' washɛːh 'ten,' ʔohnékahtɛːtyɔːh 'the water is flowing.' No word spoken in isolation ends in a vowel, and words that may seem to end in one have in reality either a final h, if the vowel gradually trails off through a whisper, or a final ʔ, if the vowel ends abruptly.

The glottal stop, written ʔ, is used by English speakers in the middle of expressions like uh uh (meaning 'no!') and for the sound represented by the t's in button, bottle, Fenton. In German, the same sound can be observed between the e and a of Beamter 'official,' between the r and e of Verein 'club,' and at the beginning of eins 'one.' In Seneca, it occurs in positions where it does not ordinarily occur in either English or German. Note ʔ in ʔoʔéohtaʔ 'plant,' keʔnyáʔkeh 'on my finger,' ʔakyέʔhis 'I make mistakes,' kaʔhnyaʔ 'stick, club,' niwákʔaːh 'how short it is.' No word spoken in isolation begins with a vowel, and words that may seem to begin with one have in reality an initial ʔ.

Several combinations of consonants, specifically sy, ty, and thy, require special comment. In all three of these, the y is pronounced with the tongue very close to the palate, producing a fricative (hissing or buzzing) sound.

The sound of the s in sy is similar to that usually spelled sh in English (for example, in show), so that the combination sy sounds more or less like what is spelled -sh y- in wash yourself. Note its sound in kaʔtaːsyoːt 'Stomp Dance.'

The combination **ty**, in which the **t** has a sound like English *d*, is apt to sound to English-speaking listeners like what is written *j* in English. Note its sound in **tyó:yaik** 'robin,' **satyɛ:h** 'sit down!' Careful listening may sometimes be necessary to distinguish it from the Seneca sound written *j*, which always sounds more like *dz*; compare the two words above with **jɛ:stáʔɛ:ʔ** 'black,' **tajɔh** 'come in!.' If a *j*-like sound occurs before **i**, it should always be written **j** (see above); **ty** never occurs before **i**.

The combination **thy** is apt to sound like the sound written *ch* in English *choose*. The **hy** of the **thy** combinaion actually has a sound similar to that which ends the German word *ich* 'I.' Note the sound of **thy** in **hothyo:wi:h** 'he has told about it,' **ʔoʔthya:taʔt** 'they (two men) stood up.' If a *ch*-like sound occurs before **i**, it should always be written **ts** (see above); **thy** never occurs before **i**.

To summarize the points of comparison with English that the reader may find useful to keep in mind in writing consonants:

For what sounds like English   *Write Seneca*

n (not word-final after Seneca ɛ or ɔ)	**n**
w	**w**
y	**y**
s, z	**s**
ch (before Seneca **i**)	**ts**
k, g, ng (if the *ng* is word-final after Seneca ɛ or ɔ)	**k**
t, d, n (if the *n* is word-final after Seneca ɛ or ɔ)	**t**
dz, j (if the *j* is before Seneca **i**)	**j**
h	**h**
glottal stop	**ʔ**
sh-y	**sy**
j (not before Seneca **i**)	**ty**
ch (not before Seneca **i**)	**thy**

There are a few Seneca nicknames in which the letters **b** or **m** must be used: **kóʔbit, takam**. The letter **u**, representing a sound something like that in German *Huhn* 'hen,' is necessary only in words that refer to something tiny: **niwúʔu:h** 'it's tiny.'

II. Grammar

"Dans leur langue, presque tout est verbe. . . ."
(J. A. Cuoq, 1866)

This section is concerned exclusively with the structure of words; no attention is given to the arrangement of words in sentences. Seneca words are complex—most must be translated by an English phrase or sentence—and even this limited aspect of the grammar can be presented only in its broad outlines if we are to maintain the simplicity that is one of the aims of this book.

It will be helpful at the outset to introduce one or two technical linguistic concepts. The very fact that this section discusses the analysis of words implies that words are not the smallest meaningful units of speech. The smallest units, the irreducible meaningful constituents of language, are termed morphemes. Morphemes are in turn represented by phonemes, the distinctive speech sounds introduced in section I. The English word *unnecessarily* contains three morphemes: *un-* "not," *-necessari-* "needful," and *-ly*, which adds an adverbial meaning to the preceding.

It may be noted that what is represented in this word by the spelling *-necessari-* is differently spoken (as well as written) in the single morpheme word *necessary*. The stresses are different, as is the sound following the *r*. These two variants are called different allomorphs of the same morpheme. There are Seneca morphemes that have 10 or more allomorphs, some of which bear no resemblance to others which nevertheless belong to the same morpheme. Which allomorph occurs in a particular word is determined by the neighboring morphemes in that word. In some environments, some morphemes occur in a zero allomorph, symbolized by ø.

Variation in the occurrence and position of vowel length (:) and accent (') will be found to occur within many morphemes. Such variation is dependent upon position within a word, as well as a number of other complex factors, and cannot be further accounted for here.

Seneca has three kinds of words or parts of speech, distin

guished by their function within sentences, as well as by their internal structure. They are particles, nouns, and verbs, and will be taken up in that order.

Particles

The particles are predominantly words of one or two morphemes, and there is consequently little or nothing to be said concerning their internal structure. Some of the most common particles include:

háeʔkwah 'also'
haʔkwístɛʔ 'something, anything'
heh 'where'
hetkɛh 'up in the air'
hɛ:nɔh 'don't!'
hɛ́:ɔweh 'where'
hɛʔɛh 'no'
hi:kɛ:h 'this one, that one, he, she, it'
ka:oʔ 'in this direction'
ka:weh 'where?'
kaɛkwah 'very'
kɛs 'repeatedly'
kwaʔ 'completely, to an extreme'
kwistɛʔ 'anything'
kyɔʔɔh 'it is said'
naeh (or nä:h) intensifies meaning
neh 'the; it, this'
neʔ 'it is, this is'
ne:waʔ 'this time'
neʔhoh 'there, that there'
nɛ:h 'this'
nɛ:tah 'this'
nɔ:h 'probably'
nɔʔwe:ʔ 'while'
sɛ:nɔh 'don't!'
sɛʔɛh 'because'
shɔ:h 'only, just'
sih 'there'
skɛ:nɔʔ 'good, well, OK'
sɔ:ka:ʔ 'somebody'
ta:h 'and' (sentence connective)
tá:ʔkwistɛʔ 'nothing'

teʔkátkaʔhoh 'nowhere'
teʔwɛ:tɔh 'never'
tɛʔɛh 'what?'
the:tɛʔ 'yesterday'
tih 'at this point, then'
to:kɛs 'in fact, yes'
waih 'indeed'
wáyɛ:ʔ 'isn't it so?'
we:ɛh 'far'
ya:eʔ 'first'
ʔá:hɔʔɔh 'most'
ʔakwas 'everywhere, wherever'
ʔasteh 'outside, outdoors'
ʔátiʔkwah 'if, whether'
ʔɛ:ʔ 'yes'
ʔi:s 'you'
ʔi:wi:h 'I think'
ʔi:ʔ 'I, we, us'
ʔónɛhjih 'a long time ago'
ʔo:nɛh 'now, at the time'
ʔɔkyeh 'inside, indoors'

Nouns

There are a few nouns which cannot be analyzed into more than one morpheme; for example, kiskwi:s 'pig,' skoʔäk 'frog.' With the exception of these and the elliptical nouns mentioned on page 13, every noun consists of a noun stem preceded by a pronominal prefix. The stem consists in turn of a noun base followed by a noun suffix, so that the relationship between the constituents can be diagramed as follows:

Pronominal prefix—Noun stem

Noun base—Noun suffix

The three noun suffixes are -ʔ (sometimes -h), whose meaning is simply to indicate that the word functions as a noun, -ʔkeh (sometimes -:neh) meaning 'on' or 'at,' and -kɔ:h, 'in' or 'under.' Their use can be illustrated with the noun base -ɔshä- 'box' and the neuter pronominal prefix ka-: káɔshäʔ 'a box,' káɔshäʔkeh 'on a box,' káɔshäkɔ:h 'in a box.'

Many of the pronominal prefixes consist of several morphemes, but they are not further analyzed here. There are two sets of pronominal prefixes that occur with noun stems. For reasons that will become clear in the discussion of the verb below, one set is called subjective and the other objective. In general, the subjective prefixes occur only with noun stems that designate things like body parts, the possession of which is inalienable. They are illustrated below with the stem -ahsiʔtaʔ 'foot':

1. k- or ke- 'my'; kahsíʔtaʔ 'my foot'
2. s-, se-, or j- 'your'; sahsíʔtaʔ 'your foot'
3. ha-,hε-, or h- 'his'; hahsíʔtaʔ 'his foot'
4. ye-, yε-, yɔ, or yak- 'her or people's'; yɔhsíʔtaʔ 'her foot' or 'people's feet'
5. ka-, kε-, k-, w-, or y- 'its'; wahsíʔtaʔ 'its foot'
6. ʔakhni-, ʔakhny-, ʔakhn-, ʔaki-, or ʔaky- 'our' (*exclusive dual; there are two of us, and you are not included*); ʔakhnyáhsiʔtaʔ 'our feet'
7. hni-, hny-, hn-, ti-, or ty- 'our' (*inclusive dual; you are included, yours and mine*) hnyahsíʔtaʔ 'our feet'
8. sni-, sny-, or sn- 'your' (*dual*); snyahsíʔtaʔ 'your feet'
9. hni-, hny-, hn-, hi-, or hy- 'their' (*masculine dual; including at least one man*); hnyahsíʔtaʔ 'their feet'
10. khni, khny-, khn-, ki-, or ky- 'their' (*nonmasculine dual; including no men*); khnyahsíʔtaʔ 'their feet'
11. ʔakwa-, ʔakwε-, ʔakw-, or ʔaky- 'our' (*exclusive plural; three or more*); ʔakwáhsiʔtaʔ 'our feet'
12. twa-, twε-, tw-, or ty- 'our' (*inclusive plural*); twahsíʔtaʔ 'our feet'
13. swa-, swε-, sw-, or j- 'your' (*plural*); swahsíʔtaʔ 'your feet'
14. hati- or hεn- 'their' (*masculine plural*); hεnɔ́hsiʔtaʔ 'their feet'
15. wati- or wεn- 'their' (*nonmasculine plural*); wεnɔ́hsiʔtaʔ 'their feet'

Other noun stems take the objective prefixes, of which there are fewer because of the coalescence of the exclusive and inclusive categories and the lack of a dual-plural distinction in the third person. The objective prefixes are illustrated below with the stem -ʔnɔʔ 'arrow':

16. ʔak- or ake- 'my'; ʔakéʔnɔʔ 'my arrow'
17. sa-, sε-, or s- 'your'; saʔnɔʔ 'your arrow'
18. ho-, haw-, or ha- 'his'; hoʔnɔʔ 'his arrow'
19. ko-, kaw-, or ka- 'her'; koʔnɔʔ 'her arrow'

20. ʔo-, ʔaw-, or ʔa- 'its' ; ʔoʔnɔʔ 'its arrow'
21. ʔɔkhni-, ʔɔkhny-, ʔɔkhn-, ʔɔki-, or ʔɔky- 'our'
    (*dual*) ʔɔkhníʔnɔʔ 'our arrow'
22. sni-, sny-, or sn- 'your' (*dual*) ; sniʔnɔʔ 'your arrow'
23. ʔɔkwa-, ʔɔkwɛ-, ʔɔkw-, or ʔɔky- 'our' (*plural*) ʔɔkwáʔnɔʔ
    'our arrow'
24. swa-, swɛ-, sw-, or j- 'your' (*plural*) ; swaʔnɔʔ 'your arrow'
25. hoti- or hon- 'their' (*masculine nonsingular; two or
    more*) ; hotíʔnɔʔ 'their arrow'
26. ʔoti- or ʔon- 'their' (*nonmasculine nonsingular*) ; ʔotíʔnɔʔ
    'their arrow'

Many noun stems occur with both prefix 5 (subjective 'its')
and prefix 20 (objective 'its'), with a difference in meaning de-
scribable as indefinite versus specific: kasnɔʔ 'bark,' ʔosnɔʔ 'the
bark.' Other stems occur consistently with either one or the
other prefix.

More complex nouns may have a base consisting of more than
a single morpheme—for example, ʔojistɔtáʔshä̇ʔ 'strawberry';
literally 'that which has an ember on it'—or may end with the
plural suffix -shɔʔ. Examples of words with the latter are
keʔnyáʔshɔʔ 'my fingers' (cf. keʔnyaʔ 'my finger'), kahatakɔ:shɔʔ
'in the forests' (cf. kahatakɔ:h 'in the forest').

Some nouns have an elliptical form, lacking the pronominal
prefix: jistɔtáʔshä̇ʔ 'strawberry,' ʔahtáhkwaʔ 'shoe.' Sometimes
the regular form with the pronominal prefix (ʔojistɔtáʔshä̇ʔ) is
also used and sometimes not (as with the word for shoe).

Verbs

Many verbs consist solely of a verb stem preceded by a pronominal prefix, which may be one of the subjective or objective
prefixes already discussed. A verb stem consists of a verb base
followed by an aspect suffix, so that the arrangement parallels
that of the nouns:

Pronominal prefix—Verb stem

Verb base—Aspect suffix

Each of these constituents may contain one or more morphemes.

Three of the four common aspect suffixes will be discussed
here, and the fourth will be taken up below. These three will be

referred to as the *descriptive, iterative,* and *imperative* suffixes. All of them have a great variety of allomorphs, and little more can be done here than to list them. The descriptive suffix occurs in the forms -ʔ, -:ʔ, -h, -:h, -ɛh, -ɔh, -ɔ:h, and -ø. It indicates that the verb base refers to a continuous state with no specific temporal limits. This state may be the result of an action denoted by the base; thus, **kothéʔtɔh,** containing the base -theʔt- 'to pound corn,' can be translated into English as either 'she is pounding corn' (with no specific end in sight) or 'she has pounded the corn.' There is less ambiguity from the point of view of an English speaker when the base is translatable as an adjective: **wi:yo:h** 'it's good, beautiful.'

The iterative suffix appears as -haʔ, -h, -aʔ, -ɔʔ, -s, -:s, -as, -ʔs, -eʔs, -ɛs, -ɔs, -ɔʔs, and ø. It indicates that the base refers either to repeated occurrences or to an occurrence that is in progress, but will eventually terminate: **yethéʔthaʔ** 'she (periodically) pounds corn' or 'she's pounding corn' (but will eventually stop). With bases translatable as adjectives, a translation expressing plurality is often called for: **wi:yoʔs** 'it's good repeatedly, several things are good.'

The imperative suffix has the forms -h, -:h, -ih, -ah, -äh, -oh, -ɛh, -t, -k, and -ø. Its meaning is one of exhortation: **säkoh** 'take it out!' **sniyɔ:tɛh** 'hang it up!'.

Except when the verb stem contains the descriptive suffix, a subjective pronominal prefix occurring before a verb stem is translatable as the subject of a verb in English; thus, **yethéʔthaʔ** 'she pounds corn,' **ha:kɛh** 'he sees (it).' Conversely, an objective prefix is translatable as an object: **ho:kɛh** 'something sees him.' With the descriptive suffix, however, the functions of these pronominal prefixes are somewhat different. The subjective prefix occurs only if the stem has an intransitive meaning, and it indicates the person or thing described: **haya:sɔh** 'he's called, his name is,' **kani:yɔ:t** 'it's hanging.' The objective prefix occurs with transitive stems and may be translated as either the subject or the object: **ho:kɛh** 'he has seen (it)' or '(something) has seen him.'

In addition to the subjective and objective prefixes, there is a third set of pronominal prefixes that occurs only with verb stems. These prefixes indicate both a subject and an object, and are termed transitive:

27.   kɔ- or kɔy- 'I . . . you (*singular*)'; kɔ:kɛh 'I see you'
28.   **khni-, khny-, khn-, ki-,** or **ky-** 'I or we (*dual*) . . . you

(*singular or dual*)'; khni:kɛh 'I, we see you.' Either subject or object (or both) is dual.

29. kwa-, kwɛ-, kw-, or ky- 'I or we (*dual or plural*) . . . you (*singular, dual or plural*)'; kwa:kɛh 'I, we see you.' Either subject or object (or both) is plural.

30. sk- or ske- 'you (*singular*) . . . me'; ske:kɛh 'you see me'

31. skhni-, skhny-, skhn-, ski-, or sky- 'you (*singular or dual*) . . . me or us (*dual*)'; skhni:kɛh 'you see me, us.' Cf. 28

32. skwa-, skwɛ-, skw-, or sky- 'you (*singular, dual or plural*) . . . me or us (*dual or plural*)'; skwa:kɛh 'you see me, us.' Cf. 29

33. he- or hey- 'I . . . him'; he:kɛh 'I see him'

34. shakhni-, shakhny-, shakhn-, shaki-, or shaky- 'we (*exclusive dual*) . . . him'; shakhni:kɛh 'we see him'

35. shakwa-, shakwɛ-, shakw-, or shaky- 'we (*exclusive plural*) . . . him'; shakwa:kɛh 'we see him'

36. shehni-, shehny-, shehn-, sheti-, or shety- 'we (*inclusive dual*) . . . him'; shehni:kɛh 'we see him'

37. shetwa-, shetwɛ-, shetw-, or shety- 'we (*inclusive plural*) . . . him'; shetwa:kɛh 'we see him'

38. hehs-, hehse-, or hej- 'you (*singular*) . . . him'; hehse:kɛh 'you see him'

39. shesni-, shesny-, or shesn- 'you (*dual*) . . . him'; shesni:kɛh 'you see him'

40. sheswa-, sheswɛ-, shesw-, or shej- 'you (*plural*) . . . him'; sheswa:kɛh 'you see him'

41. howɔ-, howɛ-, howɔy-, or how- 'he, she, or they . . . him'; howɔ:kɛh 'he, she, they see him'

42. khe- or khey- 'I . . . her or them'; khe:kɛh 'I see her, them'

43. ʔakhi- or ʔakhiy- 'we (*exclusive nonsingular*) . . . her or them'; ʔakhi:kɛh 'we see her, them'

44. ʔethi- or ʔethiy- 'we (*inclusive nonsingular*) . . . her or them'; ʔethi:kɛh 'we see her, them'

45. she- or shey- 'you (*singular*) . . . her or them'; she:kɛh 'you see her, them'

46. ʔetsi- or ʔetsiy- 'you (*nonsingular*) . . . her or them'; ʔetsi:kɛh 'you see her, them'

47. hak- or hake- 'he . . . me'; hake:kɛh 'he sees me'

48. shɔkhni-, shɔkhny-, shɔkhn-, shɔki-, or shɔky- 'he . . . us (*dual*)'; shɔkhni:kɛh 'he sees us'

49. shɔkwa-, shɔkwɛ-, shɔkw-, or shɔky- 'he . . . us (*plural*)'; shɔkwa:kɛh 'he sees us'

50. ya- or yɛ- 'he . . . you (*singular*)'; ya:kɛh 'he sees you'
51. shesni-, shesny-, or shesn- 'he . . . you (*dual*)'; shesni:kɛh 'he sees you'
52. sheswa-, sheswɛ-, shesw-, or shej- 'he . . . you (*plural*)'; sheswa:kɛh 'he sees you'
53. shako-, shakaw-, or shaka- 'he . . . her'; shako:kɛh 'he sees her'
54. hakɔ- or hakɔy-'he . . . them'; hakɔ:kɛh 'he sees them'
55. ʔɔk- or ʔɔke- 'she . . . me'; ʔɔke'kɛh 'she sees me'
56. ʔesa-, ʔesɛ-, or ʔes- 'she . . . you (*singular*)'; ʔesa:kɛh 'she sees you'
57. hɔk- or hɔke-'they . . . me'; hɔke:kɛh 'they see me'
58. hɔsa-, hɔsɛ-, or hɔs- 'they . . . you (*singular*)'; hɔsa:kɛh 'they see you'
59. ʔɔkhi- or ʔɔkhiy- 'she or they . . . us'; ʔɔkhi:kɛh 'she, they see us'
60. ʔetsi- or ʔetsiy- 'she or they . . . you (*nonsingular*)'; ʔetsi:kɛh 'she, they see you'
61. shakoti- or shakon- 'they (*masculine*) . . . her'; shakoti:kɛh 'they see her'
62. hɔwɔti- or hɔwɛn- 'she or they . . . them (*masculine*)'; hɔwɔti:kɛh 'she, they see them'
63. kɔwɔti- or kɔwɛn- 'she or they . . . them (*nonmasculine*)'; kɔwɔti:kɛh 'she, they see them'
64. kɔwɔ- or kɔwɔy- 'it . . . it'; kɔwɔ:kɛh 'it sees it'

The meaning 'he . . . him,' which may be expressed by prefix 41, may also be expressed by the objective prefix 18. 'She . . . her' may be expressed either by prefix 19 or by the forms yɔtat-, yɔtah-, or yɔtate-, which are actually prefix 4 plus a reciprocal morpheme. The latter forms may also mean 'they (*nonmasculine*) . . . her.' Neuter subjects are normally implied in the various objective prefixes, neuter objects in the subjective prefixes. The meanings of prefixes 5, 20, and 64 thus overlap.

The verb structure described above may be expanded in a number of different ways. The verb base may occur with a noun base before it, most commonly to denote its object, but sometimes its subject or an instrument: hanähtakɛh 'he sees a leaf' (-näht[a]- 'leaf'); kanähtɛʔs 'a leaf falls'; haʔhnyáyɛthaʔ 'he hits it with a club' (-ʔhnya- 'club').

The verb base may also begin with the reflexive morpheme, indicating that the subject is affected by whatever is described, or with the reciprocal, indicating that the subject acts upon itself.

Note the reflexive -at- in ꞌakatihíkwä:ɔh 'I've put my hat on'—cf. ꞌakihikwâ:ɔh 'I've put a hat on it'—the reciprocal -atat- in ꞌoꞌkátathe:ꞌ 'I cut myself.'

Morphemes may be suffixed to the base to add causative, inchoative, distributive, instrumental, dative, and other meanings. Causative -ht- occurs in honɔ́hehtɔh 'he has filled it' (-nɔhe- 'be full'). Inchoative -ꞌ- occurs in ꞌoꞌkyɛ:teꞌt 'I came to know it' (-yɛte- 'know'). Distributive -hɔ- occurs in hanéꞌakhɔh 'he does a number of wrong things' (-neꞌak- 'do wrong'). Instrumental -hkw- occurs in ꞌohsóhkwaꞌ 'it's used for coloring, paint' (-hso- 'color'). Dative -ni- occurs in hakhyatɔ:ni:h 'he has written it for me' (-hyatɔ- 'write'). All these morphemes have several other allomorphs.

The aspect suffix may also be modified to indicate progression, continuation, past time, and several other meanings. The progressive morpheme -atye- occurs in hothyówi:atyeꞌ 'he was talking along about it.' Continuative -ak- occurs in ꞌɛyétheꞌtha:k 'she'll continue to pound corn.' The past morpheme -kwaꞌ occurs in hanɔ́eꞌskwaꞌ 'he used to like it.'

Another group of suffixes may add an attributive meaning to the entire word:

-ko:wa:h 'big, great, important'; hatíyosko:wa:h 'he's a great fighter'

-ꞌah 'almost, kind of'; ꞌoꞌkâ:sꞌah 'it's almost night, evening'

-kha:ꞌ, -ke:aꞌ, -kaꞌ, or -ka:ꞌ 'characterized by, the . . . variety'; ꞌɔkwéꞌɔwe:kha:ꞌ 'the Indian variety, the Seneca language'

-:onɔꞌ 'person of or from'; tkanɔtasé:onɔꞌ 'person from Newtown' (on the Cattaraugus Reservation)

-kɛ:ɔꞌ 'former, deceased'; haksótkɛ:ɔꞌ 'my deceased grandfather'

-shɔꞌɔh 'pluralization'; howéshɔꞌɔh 'his belongings'—cf. ho:wɛh 'it belongs to him'

The verb may also be modified by the addition of prefixes. In many cases, the form of the pronominal prefix will then be a variant, but these variations are too numerous to be listed here. Especially common are the future, indicative, and optative prefixes. A verb which contains one of these commonly ends with a fourth aspect suffix, the punctual; this is the only condition under which the punctual suffix occurs. The forms of the punctual suffix are exactly like those of the imperative (p. 14), except that wherever the imperative has h, the punctual has ꞌ. It means that whatever is referred to by the verb base happens only once.

The future prefix occurs as ʔɛ- or ʔe- and has a future meaning: ʔɛke:kɛʔ 'I'll see it.' Another example was given with the continuative morpheme above. The indicative has the forms ʔoʔ-, wa-, or ʔe-, and means that the event is an incontestable fact. It is often, although not necessarily, translated with the simple past tense in English: ʔoʔke:kɛʔ 'I saw it' or 'I see it' (*right at this moment*). Other examples were given with the reciprocal and inchoative morphemes above. The optative prefix occurs in the forms ʔa:- or ʔae- and indicates likelihood or obligation: ʔa:ke:kɛʔ 'I might see it' or 'I ought to see it.'

The verb structure described, whether or not it is modified by one of the three prefixes just listed, may also be preceded by one or more of several other prefixes. Among these are the following:

t- or **ti-** 'there, here, this way'; **tkã:hkwitkɛʔs** 'the sun emerges there, the east.'

he-, h-, or **haʔ-** 'over there, that way'; **heyakawe:nɔ:h** 'she has gone over there'

s-, t-, or **ji-** 'again, back, other, one'; **shata:kheʔ** 'he's running again'

te-, t-, or **ti-** 'duplication, change of state'; **tejitwatas** 'let's stand it back up'

teʔ-, te-, or **taʔ-** 'negation'; **teʔwi:yo:h** 'it's not good'

ni-, n-, or **nɔʔ-** 'how'; **nikye:haʔ** 'how I do it'

tsi-, ts-, or **tsaʔ-** 'when'; **tsikeksaʔá:h** 'when I was a small child'

thi-, th-, thaʔ- 'contrast'; **thiyókweʔta:teʔ** 'it's a different person'

III. Glossary

"Nor is it always easy to comprehend or state with precision the shade of meaning implied in the Indian word." (H. M. Lloyd, 1901)

The terms presented in this section are arranged according to categories, since it was felt that such an arrangement would be considerably more useful than an alphabetical one. The categories are listed in the table of contents. The English equivalents are listed alphabetically in the index.

Each entry lists the Seneca term, variant spellings used by other writers (identified by abbreviations—p. 59), English equivalents, also followed by abbreviations if peculiar to a particular source, and a literal translation when one is known and when the English equivalents are not literal translations.

A few words regarding these literal translations are necessary. Many terms in the glossary refer to some specific cultural item, but have at the same time a descriptive meaning that is apparent to any speaker of Seneca; for example, keɔtanɛhkwih 'horse' means literally 'it hauls logs.' Other terms, like kaˀta:syo:t, usually translated 'stomp dance' by the Indians, have historical meanings not recognized by most or all present-day speakers. That this particular term originated with the meaning 'standing quiver' is not apparent to many speakers today, presumably because people have ceased talking about quivers. Other terms contain features that defy satisfactory interpretation. While speculation on such items is always possible and occasionally rewarding, only those meanings which have been apparent to Seneca speakers or which are reasonably certain etymologically have been given.

1. Classifications of Society

A. Kinship Terminology

The stem -nɔ:k means 'be (*either consanguineally or affinally*) related to':

he:nɔ:k 'I'm related to him'
she:nɔ:k 'you're related to her, them'
ˀakwatɛ:nɔ:k 'we (*exclusive plural*) are related to each other'
etc.

The system described in the rest of this section is the traditional Seneca classification, which is actually familiar today to only a minority of the older people. In the context of this classification, the English kinship terms such as *cousin, mother* etc., which are customarily used by both ethnologists and Indians as translations of the Seneca terms, are necessarily only rough labels, not to be understood in the meanings which they have in reference to our own kinship system. The latter system is also recognized by the Indians, of course, and the English translations are accurate for the Seneca terms when they are employed in the context of this latter system.

A few observations on the linguistic peculiarities exhibited by these terms may be helpful. Nearly all the kinship terms consist of a verb stem denoting a particular relationship, preceded by a pronominal prefix that specifies the member or members of the relationship referred to. In general, stems that denote relationships between members of the same generation, when their relative ages are not significant, occur with dual or plural subjective prefixes to denote all the members of the relationship to whom reference is made: ʔakwã:ʔse:ʔ 'we (*exclusive plural*) are cousins' (often translated 'my cousins'). For most of the relationships involving an older and a younger member, there is a stem that occurs with transitive prefixes of which the subject is the older, the object the younger member: -ʔkɛʔ 'to be an older sibling of, to have as a younger sibling' in, for example, heʔkɛʔ 'I am his older sibling, my younger brother.' While stems of this type can refer to either the older or younger member, they are more commonly used to refer only to the younger member of the relationship, another stem being more commonly used to refer to the older. These last stems are, from the point of view of other verb stems in the language, irregular with regard to the meaning, form, or both, of some of the pronominal prefixes with which they occur:

(*a*) With some, but not all of these stems, only a singular subjective prefix is used for the terms translatable as 'my ...': hahjiʔ '(*he is*) my older brother.'

(*b*) The feminine morpheme has the form ʔa-: ʔahjiʔ '(*she is*) my older sister.'

(*c*) Terms translatable with a second or third person possessor ('your ...', 'his ...' etc.) contain simply the appropriate second or third person objective prefix, but with the following semantic peculiarities:

ho- means 'his' or 'her' as long as one of the kinsmen involved in the relationship is male: **hohji?** 'his older brother or sister, her older brother.'

?o- means 'her' when the referent is female, but 'its' when the referent is male: **?ohji?** 'her older sister,' but **?o?nih** 'its father.'

(d) Transitive prefixes also occur, overlapping some of the meanings accounted for above, but with no consistent direction of relationship: **ya?nih** 'your father,' but **howɔ́?nih** 'their father.'

Consanguineal Kinship[1]

Kinsmen of the same generation: 'siblings.' The relationship between members of the same generation who either have a common parent or whose parents are consanguineally related, provided these related parents are of the same sex, is referred to with the stem -**atέ:nɔ:te:?** (with the duplicative prefix) 'be siblings.' Persons so related to me are, in English terms, my brothers and sisters and all my cousins in my generation, no matter of what degree, whose fathers are related to my father or whose mothers are related to my mother. Examples of this stem:

teyakyatέ:nɔ:te:? 'we (*exclusive dual*) are siblings'

teyakwatέ:nɔ:te:? [*da-yä'-gwä-dan'-no-dä*] 'we (*exclusive plural*) are siblings'

te:yátɛ:nɔ:te:? 'they (*masculine dual*) are siblings'

tɛ:notέ:nɔ:te:? 'they (*masculine plural*) are siblings'

There is also a narrower classification which distinguishes the relative age of the 'siblings.' One of the two stems used here is -**?kɛ:?** 'have as younger sibling,' and it occurs with the transitive prefixes in regular fashion:

he?kɛ:? [*ha'-ga*] 'I have him as younger sibling, my younger brother'

khe?kɛ:? [*ka'-ga*] 'I have her as younger sibling, my younger sister'

hakέ?kɛ:? 'he has me as younger sibling, my older brother'

twatáte?kɛ:? 'we (*inclusive plural*) are to each other as older

---

[1] This section follows Floyd G. Lounsbury's unpublished analysis of Iroquois consanguineal classes. The variant spellings given in brackets are all from Morgan's *Systems of Consanguinity and Affinity of the Human Family*.

to younger siblings, our younger brothers'—used to refer to white men

The other stem is the irregular -hji? 'have as older sibling':
hahji? [hä'-je] 'my older brother'
?ahji? [ah'-je] 'my older sister'

Twins are referred to with the stem -khɛh (with the duplicative prefix):

te:ni:khɛh or te:ikhɛh 'they (*masculine dual*) are twins'
tekhni:khɛh or teki:khɛh [ta-geek'-ha] 'they (*masculine dual*) are twins'

tekhni:khɛh or teki:khɛh [ta-geek'-hă] 'they (*nonmasculine dual*) are twins'

Kinsmen of the same generation: 'cousins.' The relationship between two members of the same generation whose parents are consanguineally related, when these related parents are not of the same sex, is referred to with the stem -ắ:?se:?—or -ɛ́:?se:? after an n—'be cousins.' Persons so related to me are, in English terms, all my cousins in my generation, no matter of what degree, whose fathers are related to my mother or whose mothers are related to my father. Examples of this stem:

?akyắ:?se:? [ah-gare'-seh] 'we (*exclusive dual*) are cousins'
yắ:?se:? 'they (*masculine dual*) are cousins'
hɛnɛ́:?se:? 'they (*masculine plural*) are cousins'

Kinsmen one generation apart: 'parents' and 'children.' The relationship between persons a generation apart in which the older member is either the natural parent of the younger, or is consanguineally related to and the same sex as one of the natural parents of the younger, is referred to with one of three stems. The first and more regular is -(h)a(:)wak 'have as child':

he:awak [ha-ah'-wuk] 'I have him as child, my son'
khe:awak [ka-ah'-wuk] 'I have her as child, my daughter'
hakha:wak 'he has me as child, my father'
shakóawak 'he has her as child, his daughter'
yatáthawak 'they (*masculine dual*) are parent-child to each other, a man and his son or daughter, a woman and her son'

The second stem, used only to refer to a 'father' in this relationship, is -?nih:
ho?nih 'his or her father'

hotí'nih 'their (*masculine nonsingular*) father'
ya'nih 'your father'
howó'nih 'her or their father'
ha'nih [*hä-nih*] 'my father'

The third stem, used only to refer to a 'mother' in this relationship, is -nó'ɛh:

honó'ɛh 'his mother'
'onó'ɛh 'her mother'
sanó'ɛh 'your mother'
shakotinó'ɛh 'their mother'

The common word for 'my mother,' however, is the anomalous no'yɛh [*no-yeh'*].

Kinsmen one generation apart: 'uncles,' 'aunts,' 'nephews,' and 'nieces.' The relationship between persons a generation apart in which the older member is consanguineally related to and the opposite sex from one of the natural parents of the younger is referred to with one of four stems. The two which occur with regular prefixes are -ɛ:wɔ:tɛ' 'be uncle to' and -hsó'neh 'be aunt to'; both are usually or always used to refer to the younger member of the relationship:

heyɛ́:wɔ:tɛ' [*ha-ya'-wan-da*] 'I'm his uncle, my nephew'
kheyɛ́:wɔ:tɛ' [*ka-ya'-wan-da*] 'I'm her uncle, my niece'
hehsɛ́:wɔ:tɛ' 'you're his uncle, your nephew'
howóyɛ:wɔ:tɛ' 'they're his uncles, their nephew'
hehsó'neh [*ha-soh'-neh*] 'I'm his aunt, my nephew'
khehsó'neh [*ka-soh'-neh*] 'I'm her aunt, my niece'
howotihsó'neh 'they're aunts to them (*masculine*), their nephews'

The other two are -nó'sɛh 'be uncle to' and -hak 'be aunt to,' used only to refer to the older member of the relationship:

hakhnó'sɛh 'my uncle'
yanó'sɛh 'your uncle'
shakóno'sɛh 'her uncle'
honó'sɛh 'his or her uncle'
'ake:hak [*ah-ga'-huc*] 'my aunt'
ya:hak 'your aunt (*said to a man*)'
'esa:hak 'your aunt (*said to a woman*)'
howɔ:hak 'his aunt or aunts'
ho:hak 'his aunt'
'o:hak 'her aunt'

Kinsmen two generations apart: 'grandparents' and 'grand-children.' The relationship between any consanguineally related kinsmen who are two generations apart is referred to with the stems -ate⁹ and -(h)so:t.

-a(:)te⁹ 'be grandparent to' occurs with transitive prefixes to denote either member of the relationship, but more commonly denotes the younger:

heya:te⁹ [*ha-yä'-da*] 'my grandson'
kheya:te⁹ [*ka-yä'-da*] 'my granddaughter'
haka:te⁹ 'my grandfather'
yate⁹ 'your grandson'
shako:te⁹ 'his granddaughter'
yatatate⁹ 'a man and his grandson or granddaughter, a woman and her grandson'

-(h)so:t 'be grandparent to' occurs with the irregular prefixes and refers only to the older member of the relationship:

hakso:t [*hoc'-sote*] 'my grandfather'
⁹akso:t [*oc'-sote*] 'my grandmother'
yahso:t 'your grandfather'
hohso:t 'his or her grandfather'
⁹ethíhso:t 'our (*inclusive*) grandmother' (*used ceremonially to refer to the moon*)

Kinsmen three or more generations apart: 'great-grand-parents' and 'great-grandchildren.' The relationship between consanguineally related kinsmen who are three or more genera-tions apart is referred to with the terms described immediately above, supplemented by the suffix -ko:wa:h:

haksótko:wa:h 'my great-grandfather'
heyáte⁹ko:wa:h 'my great-grandson'

Affinal Kinship

The common word for 'my spouse' is teyakyati:h 'we (*exclu-sive dual*) together make up the total.' Also frequently used are hekéhjih 'my husband,' literally 'my old man,' and khekéhjih 'my wife, my old lady.' Less standardized, often facetious forms are sometimes used by particular individuals; for example, teyakyatkɔɛtáhkwa⁹ 'we lay down our heads together.' In refer-ring to another person's spouse the usual word is né:yo⁹ 'his or her spouse.' The verb stem -hyo:⁹ 'be man and wife' occurs regu-larly with the reciprocal in such words as yata:thyo:⁹ 'he and his wife.' There is also a noun stem -nóhkwa⁹ found in kanɔ́hkwaʔ 'married couple,' honɔ́hkwaʔ 'his wife,' konɔ́hkwaʔ 'her husband.'

Kinsmen of the same generation: 'brothers-in-law' and 'sisters-in-law.' The relationship between affinally related kinsmen of the same generation is referred to with three different stems: -a(:)tyoh, -ãʔni:eʔ, and -a(:)nyɛh. The differences in meaning between these stems are not entirely clear, since the terms are little used today, and Morgan's information is somewhat confusing. The following is based on Morgan, with alternative meanings from present-day speakers given in the footnotes.

-a(:)tyoh is used when the kinsmen are of the same sex:[1]

ʔakya:tyoh [ah-ge-äh'-ne-o (?)] 'we (exclusive dual) are brothers-in-law or sisters-in-law, my brother-in-law (said by a man), my sister-in-law (said by a woman)'

yatyoh 'your brother-in-law (said to a man), your sister-in-law (said to a woman)'

-ãʔni:eʔ is used by a man to refer to a woman:

ʔakãʔni:eʔ [ah-ge-ah'-ne-ah] 'my sister-in-law' (said by a man)

-a(:)nyɛh seems to have the same meaning[2] and is not given by Morgan:

ʔakya:nyɛh 'my sister-in-law'

Morgan gives in addition the terms ha-yă'-o and ka-yă'-o, used respectively by a woman to refer to a man and vice versa. Perhaps these are heyɛ́ɔʔ 'I set him down' and kheyɛ́ɔʔ 'I set her down.'

Another stem which indicates an affinal relationship between members of the same generation is -atɛno:ɔʔ. This, however, is used to refer to the relationship between sets of parents who are related through the marriage of their children:

ʔakwatɛno:ɔʔ 'we are parents-in-law of the same couple'

Kinsmen one generation apart: 'parents-in-law' and 'children-in-law.' The relationship between affinally related kinsmen a generation apart is referred to with the stems -e:hɔ:s, -ne:hɔ:s, and -saʔ.

-e:hɔ:s is used reciprocally to refer to the relationship between a son-in-law and his parents-in-law:

ʔakhne:hɔ:s [oc-na'-hose] 'we (exclusive dual) are related as

---

[1] But current evidence suggests that it is used when at least one of the kinsmen is male.

[2] Or else it is used only to refer to a female kinsman.

son-in-law to parent-in-law'
ʔakweːhɔːs 'we (*exclusive plural*) ...'

-ne(ː)hɔːs 'have as son-in-law' occurs with transitive prefixes and the reciprocal prefix:
shakhnínehɔːs 'our son-in-law'
yatáhnehɔːs 'he or she and his or her son-in-law'

-saʔ 'have as daughter-in-law' occurs with transitive prefixes to refer to either member of this relationship:
kheːsaʔ [*kaʹ-sä*] 'my daughter-in-law'
sheːsaʔ 'your daughter-in-law'
hakeːsaʔ [*hä-gaʹ-sä*] 'my father-in-law' (*said by a woman*)
ʔɔkeːsaʔ [*on-gaʹ-sä*] 'my mother-in-law' (*said by a woman*)
kosaʔ 'her daughter-in-law'

The stems -noː? and -nɔ́ʔis are used in referring to a step-parent-stepchild relationship.

-noː? 'have as stepchild' occurs with transitive prefixes to denote either member of this relationship, but more commonly refers to the younger:
heːnoː? [*haʹ-no*] 'my stepson'
kheːnoː? [*kaʹ-no*] 'my stepdaughter'
hakhno:? 'my stepfather'
hɔwɔːnoː? 'her, their stepson'

-nɔ́ʔis 'be stepparent to' occurs with irregular prefixes and refers only to the older member of the relationship:
hakhnɔ́ʔis [*hoc-noʹ-ese*] 'my stepfather'
ʔakhnɔ́ʔis [*oc-noʹ-ese*] 'my stepmother'
honɔ́ʔis 'his stepfather or stepmother, her stepfather'
ʔonɔ́ʔis 'her stepmother'

B. Other Social Classifications

The Family

The noun stem -(h/ː)wajiːyäʔ 'family' occurs with subjective pronominal prefixes and is used now to refer to the kinsmen with whom one resides, although historical sources indicate that it earlier referred to a matrilineage:[1]
khwajiːyäʔ 'my family'
haːwajiːyäʔ 'his family'
yeːwajiːyäʔ 'her family'

---

[1] See J. N. B. Hewitt, *Bureau of American Ethnology Annual Report* 21, p. 255, footnote a (1903).

Clans

The word for 'clan' ('tribe'—LHM) is **kaʔsä:teʔ**; witn the distributive morpheme, **kaʔsä:te:nyɔʔ** 'the clans.' The morpheme **-ʔsä:-** 'clan' is found in numerous other words.

The names of the eight matrilineal clans are listed below with the pronominal prefixes denoting 'they are members of the . . . clan.' With the exception of the Turtle Clan, the names bear no relation to the common names of the respective animals, although Morgan listed principally the latter.

hotijɔníʔka:ʔ 'they are Bears'
honɔtha:yɔ:nih 'they are Wolves,' often simply **thá:yɔ:nih**
    [*tor-yoh'-ne*—*LHM*]
hatínyahtɛ:h 'they are Turtles'
hotíkɛʔke:ka:ʔ 'they are Beavers'
hotí:nyɔkwaiyoʔ 'they are Deer'
hotíswɛʔkaiyoʔ 'they are Hawks'
hotíʔnehsi:yoʔ 'they are Snipes'
honɔtáɛʔɔ:ka:ʔ or **hotitáɛʔɔ:ka:ʔ** 'they are Herons'

There is also a term for the members of 'my father's clan': **ʔakatɔní:onɔʔ**, literally 'the people from whom I have grown, who engendered me.'

Moieties

The two moieties are not named. In Reservation English they are usually referred to as 'sides.' The first four clans listed above are sometimes called 'the animal side,' the last four 'the bird side.' The members of the same moiety share a relationship expressed by the stem **-atɛ:nɔtyɔʔshɔʔ**, an expansion of the base that means 'to be brothers and sisters,' while the relationship between the members of opposite moieties is expressed by the stem **-ä:ʔse:shɛʔ**, an expansion of the base that means 'to be cousins':

ʔakwatɛ:nɔtyɔʔshɔʔ 'we (*exclusive plural*) belong to the same moiety'
honɔtɛ:nɔtyɔʔshɔʔ 'they (*masculine*) belong to the same moiety'
ʔɔkwä:ʔséshɛʔ 'we belong to opposite moieties'
honɛ:ʔséshɛʔ 'they belong to opposite moieties'

Nations

The term for the 'Six Nations' is **ye:iʔ níonɔɛjake:h**, literally 'six lands.'

Grouping by Age and Sex

A community may be further thought of as divided into the following four classes of people:

yeksá'shɔ'ɔh or hatiksa'shɔ'ɔh 'the children'
wɛniɔshɔ'ɔh 'the women'
hotiskɛ'ɛkehtɔh 'the warriors'
yekɛhjishɔ'ɔh or hatikɛhjíshɔ'ɔh 'the old people'

The women, as a group, may also be referred to as 'akhíno'ɛh, literally 'our mothers.'

C. Functionaries

Longhouse Officials

Members of the longhouse community are called kanɔhseské:onɔ' 'longhouse people.' Their principal appointed officials are honɔti:ɔt 'Faith Keepers' (WNF), 'head ones, fire keepers' (RE), literally 'appointed ones.' A single 'Faith Keeper' is a hotí:ɔt if a man, a kotí:ɔt if a woman. At Allegany and Cattaraugus there are particular 'Faith Keepers' who have more authority than the others. They may be called hatíhsɛnowanɛh 'chiefs' (see Civil Officials below) or, at Cattaraugus, 'óɛtɔshɔ' 'head ones.' A head woman at Cattaraugus may be called kotókɛstɔh 'she keeps it straight.' At Allegany there are two male 'Faith Keepers' with special duties who are known as honɔti:wáke:ɔ' 'Wampum Keepers,' literally 'they peddle the message.' A single 'Wampum Keeper' is called hoti:wáké:ɔ'.

Civil Officials

Civil leaders at Cattaraugus are called teyɔkhiya'towéhtanih 'they deliberate for us,' kowanɔ'ta' 'great one,' or hakyá'tanɔh 'he watches over me.'

At Tonawanda the chief system described by Morgan is retained. A chief (or sachem) is called hahsɛnowa:nɛh 'his name is great.' Other, less common, designations are:

hoya:ne:h, literally 'he is of noble lineage'
kaktéäkwɛni:yo', literally 'the main root'
teyɔtɔɛjayáshɔhkwa', literally 'serving the fame of the nation'

A subchief, or person next in line for the chief's title, may be called:

sho:nɔ'ne:t, literally 'he's next in line'

ʔoktéä́ʔké ha:at, literally 'he's standing on the root over there'
hɛɔtanɔh, literally 'he watches over the tree'

A third-level chief (or "messenger") is called tɛ́:hta:s, literally 'he runs.'

The eight chief titles held by the Seneca are:

kanyotaiyoʔ or skanyotaiyoʔ 'Handsome Lake'
tsaʔtekɛ́ɔye:s or shaʔtekɛ́ɔye:s 'even with the sky' or 'skies equal in length'
shokɛ́ʔjo:wa:ʔ 'he of the large forehead'
kaʔnokaeh (apparently containing the morpheme which means 'arrow')
níshanye:nɛʔt 'the two of them staggered' (elliptical)
shatyenɔwɔʔs 'he who helps' (elliptical)
kanɔhkí:ʔtawiʔ (perhaps with a meaning that involved 'frying')
to:nihokä̃:ʔwɛh (apparently containing a verb stem that means 'open')

2. Communal Activities

A. Calendrical Ceremonies

The annual ceremonies held in or centering at the longhouse are variously referred to in English as 'festivals' (LHM), 'ceremonies' (WNF), 'dances' or 'doings' (RE). The individual ceremonies are referred to in Seneca with the following terms:

kaiwanɔɔskwáʔko:wa:h [gi'-ye-wä-no-us-quä-go-wä—LHM]
'Midwinter or New Year's Ceremony.' This word has the suffix -ko:wa:h 'great, important' added to kaiwanóɔskwaʔ, a form that is not now recognized as a word, but that seems etymologically to have meant 'the matter used to be difficult,' possibly with reference to 'dream guessing.'

kanɛ́ʔyasʔɔ:ʔ (identical with the preceding). The verb base -nɛʔy- 'have the Midwinter Ceremony' may occur with various prefixes and suffixes; for example, hotínɛʔyas 'they are having the Midwinter Ceremony,' ʔɔkwanɛʔyáhseʔ 'we are going to have the Midwinter Ceremony.'

ta:tinɔ́:nyɔ wahtaʔ 'Maple or Sap Ceremony,' literally 'they are thankful for the maple.' This and many of the following terms may occur with various prefixes and suffixes; for example tɛɔtinɔ́:nyɔ:ʔ wahtaʔ 'they will be thankful for the maple, will have the Maple Ceremony.'

ta:tinɔ́:nyɔ kahatayɛˀ (identical with the preceding), literally 'they are thankful for the forest'

hɛnɔtsiskóaˀ (identical with the two preceding), literally 'they put mush in water'; that is, 'they boil mush'

ta:tinɔ́:nyɔ kä́:hkwa:ˀ 'Sun Ceremony,' literally 'they are thankful for the sun'

tɔ:wɔtínɔ:ɔnyɔ hatiwɛnotatyeˀs 'Thunder Ceremony,' literally 'they thank them, the Thunderers'

hɔwɔtiyɛnɔkóhtani hatiwɛnotatyeˀs (identical with the preceding), literally 'they put in a song for them, the Thunderers'

wasa:seˀ (identical with the two preceding), literally 'War Dance,' a component of the ceremony (cf. p. 31)

henɔhnɛɔkwaˀsyóaˀ or hɛnɔhnɛ:kwaˀsyóaˀ 'Seed or Planting Ceremony,' literally 'they put seeds in water,' evidently with reference to soaking the seeds before planting.

ˀata:yéoɔˀ 'Strawberry Ceremony,' literally 'the gathering of berries'

hɛnɔta:yé:es (identical with the preceding), literally 'they gather berries'

hɛnɔta:yo:s or hɛnɔta:yóaˀ (identical with the preceding), literally 'they put berries in water'

hɛnɔtetkɔwɔˀséoaˀ 'Bean or String Bean Ceremony,' literally 'they put (string) beans in water'

ˀatekhwéoɔˀ 'Green Corn Ceremony,' literally 'the gathering of food'

hɛnɔtekhwé:es (identical with the preceding), literally 'they gather food'

ˀathähkwéoɔˀ 'Harvest or Bread Ceremony,' literally 'the gathering of bread'

hɛnɔthähkwé:es (identical with the preceding), literally 'they gather bread'

B. Terms Associated with the Calendrical Ceremonies

The Four Rituals

The ke:i niyóiwa:ke:h 'Four Rituals' ('Four Sacred Ceremonies'—WNF) prescribed by the Creator are:

1. ˀostówäˀko:wa:h [o-sto-weh'-go-wä—LHM] 'Great Feather Dance'
   kanɔnyowa:nɛh (identical with the preceding), literally 'big dance'

2. **konéɔɔʔ** [*gä-na'-o-uh*—LHM] 'Thanksgiving, Skin, or Drum Dance,' 'Worship Dance' (RE)

3. **ʔatɔ:wɛʔ** [*ah-do'-weh*—LHM] 'Personal Chant'
   hatɔ:thaʔ 'he is singing ʔatɔ:wɛʔ'
   hɛnɔtɔishɛthaʔ 'they are accompanying ʔatɔ:wɛʔ' (saying heʔ, heʔ, heʔ in rhythm)

4. **kajéʔkekha:ʔ** 'Bowl, Dish, or Peach Stone Game,' literally 'characterized by a bowl'
   kanɛ:hwéʔko:wa:h (identical with the preceding)
   kayɛtowa:nɛh (identical with the two preceding), literally 'big game'
   kajɛʔ 'bowl'
   kaskéʔɛʔ [*gus-kä'-eh*—LHM] 'peach stone'

Songs and Dances

wasa:seʔ [*wä-sä-seh*—LHM] 'War Dance' ('Sioux War Dance' —LHM)
waɛnɛníʔje:ʔ 'they do the War Dance' (with reference to the dance step of the preceding)
waʔɛnɔʔe:ʔ [*wä-a-no'-a*—LHM] 'Striking a Stick' ('Sun Dance' —RE)
yɔthɔwi:sas, wɛnɔthɔwi:sas, or **thɔwi:sas** [*un-to-we'-sus*— LHM] 'Women's Song' (WNF), 'Shuffle Dance' (LHM), 'Sisters of the Dio 'he'ko' (ACP; see **tyɔhéhkɔh,** p. 49)
kanɔeo:wi:ʔ 'Dawn Song' ('song to the middle pantheon'— WNF)
ʔɛ:skä:nye:ʔ or **ʔɛ:hsíʔtakä:nye:ʔ** 'Women's Shuffle Dance'
ʔɛ:skä:nyé:ʔko:wa:h 'Great Shuffle Dance'
ʔɛ:skä:nye:ʔ kaɛnɔkáyɔkha:ʔ 'Old-Fashioned Shuffle Dance'
ʔonéɔʔ ʔoɛnɔʔ 'Corn Dance'
kaʔta:syo:t [*gä-dä'-shote*—LHM] 'Stomp Dance' ('Trotting Dance'—LHM), literally 'standing quiver'
teyɔtɛnéshɔthaʔ [*da-yun'-da-nes-hunt-hä*—LHM] 'Linking Arms Dance'
kanɔʔjitkɛ:ɔʔ [*gä'-no-jit'-ga-o*—LHM] 'Taking the Kettle Out' (LHM), 'Carry-Out-the-Kettle' (WNF)
kaʔnokɛ:yɔ:ʔ 'Grinding the Arrow'
(ʔo) jíhayaʔ 'Devil Dance, Devil's Feather Dance'

The last four are sometimes known collectively as the 'Devil's Four Rituals.'

Other Terms

kanɔ:nyɔk 'Thanksgiving Speech'

kaiwawéthahɔh 'Inserted Message'

hatiksaʔtóaʔ 'they are naming children,' literally 'putting children in water'

shɛnɔtathéwathaʔ 'they are confessing,' literally 'punishing themselves again'

yaté:yɛɔʔ 'Big Heads' ('Uncles'—RE)

C. Noncalendrical Ceremonies

Restricted (Medicine Ceremonies)

The following are ceremonies in which participation is, at least ideally, restricted to the members of a particular society:

nyakwaiʔ ʔoɛnɔʔ [ne-ä'-gwi—LHM] 'Bear Dance,' literally 'bear song'

tekiyáʔkɔh ʔoɛnɔʔ [da-ge'-ya-go—LHM] 'Buffalo Dance'

táwɛ:ɛtɔʔ ʔoɛnɔʔ 'Otter Dance'

kakóhsaʔ [gä-go'-sä—LHM] 'False-Face'

hotikɔhsóskaʔah 'Common Faces' ('Doctors' Dance'—ACP), literally 'they have nothing but faces' (said to be thus called because the masks lack a tobacco pouch attached to the back)

teyɔtyɔhkéothaʔ 'Thumbs-Up Dance,' literally 'they put their thumbs up'

teyɛ:hsiʔtatías 'Alternate Feet Dance' (Doorkeepers' Dance'— ACP), literally 'they alternate their feet'

teyé:nyothaʔ (part of the preceding), literally 'they stand it upright'

kajíhsaʔ 'Husk-Face'

nika:nekáʔa:h 'Little Water'

yéiʔto:s, yíːʔto:s, hatíːʔto:s, káiʔtowa:nɛh, or káiʔto:ɔʔ 'Shake the Pumpkin' (RE), 'Society of Mystic Animals' (ACP), 'Sharp Point' (WNF)

kane:nyóʔtɔːʔ (an uncommon variant of the preceding[ʔ])

kahatiyáʔkɔʔɔh 'Crossing the Woods'

hatihati:yaʔs (identical with the preceding), literally 'they cross the woods'

ka:yowéoɔʔko:wa:h (identical with the two preceding)

kaɛnɔwéthahɔh 'Inserted Song'

teyótahsɔtaikɔh [da-yo-dä'-sun-dä-e'-go—LHM] 'Dark Dance,' literally 'it's dark'

tewɛnɔtahsɔtáiktha^ʔ (identical with the preceding), literally
'they make it dark'

yí:ɔta:ʔtha^ʔ 'Quavering,' literally 'they make the words (or
voices) tremble'

(ʔo)téswate:nyɔ^ʔ [*da-swä-da-ne'-a*—LHM] 'Changing Ribs'
('Tumbling Dance'—LHM, 'Woman's Society'—ACP)

kané^ʔkwä:ʔe:^ʔ 'Eagle Dance'

kané^ʔɔta:ʔtɔh (identical with the preceding), literally 'shaking
the Eagle Dance fan'

ke:i niwáhsɔta:ke:h 'Four Nights' (performed in Canada only)

sawanó:nɔ^ʔɔ:^ʔ (an obsolete dance)

kayɛtó:ʔke:a^ʔ (also obsolete)

Unrestricted

The following ceremonies are open to the whole community:

káiwi:yo:h 'Good Message' ('Code of Handsome Lake')

ʔɛ́ɔwohsa:tɔ:^ʔ 'his funeral,' literally 'they will bury him';
ʔɛshakotíhsatɔ:^ʔ 'her funeral'

ʔatyä:khɔ:shä^ʔ 'Tenth Day Feast'

ʔohki:we:h 'Dance for the Dead' (LHM), 'Chanters for the
Dead' (ACP), 'Feast of the Dead, Ghost Dance' (WNF)

kayɛtɔ:ʔshä^ʔ (an all-night dance for the dead, commonly the all-
night version of the preceding)

kahsá^ʔɔ:^ʔ 'All Eaten Up' (another ceremony for the dead)

kanóɔhkwa:nyɔk 'Expressions of Love' (similar to the preceding, but with an offering of cider)

D. Terms Associated with the Noncalendrical Ceremonies

ʔotɛ:shä^ʔ 'medicine ceremony, dance, doings'

hotɛs 'there's a ceremony for him' ('recipient'—WNF)

hotésyɔ:ni:h 'he's preparing the ceremony' ('sponsor'—WNF)

hotésyo^ʔ 'he has the ceremony ready,' literally 'he has the ceremony in the water' ('sponsor'—WNF)

hastéistha^ʔ 'he arranges' ('conductor'—WNF)

hatyáswas 'he notifies' ('messenger'—WNF)

haya^ʔtɔtáhkɔh 'he's entitled to the ceremony' (that is, 'he belongs to the appropriate society')

yeya^ʔtɔtáhkɔh 'she's entitled to the ceremony'

hɛnéyɔ:^ʔ 'fortune teller' (male)

yɛnéyɔ:^ʔ 'fortune teller' (female)

ta:ya^ʔtówetha^ʔ 'fortune teller,' literally 'he deliberates'

ʔotsinɔhkέʔtaʔ 'charm'

honɔtsinɔ́hkɛʔ 'they belong to a charm society' ('charm holders' —WNF)

yɔtáʔsäthaʔ 'goods distributed during ʔohki:we:h'

hahoanɔ́sta:s 'he guards the door, doorkeeper'

hatíyɛʔkwayɛ:nih 'they're holding a Little Water ceremony,' literally 'putting down tobacco for it'

hatinotayɛ:nih (identical with the preceding), literally 'they're putting down a reed for it'

kano:taʔ 'night song of the Little Water society' (ACP), literally 'reed'

hatɛ:ne:t 'keeper of the Little Water medicine'

E. Secular Songs and Dances

While some of the following are performed as parts of religious ceremonies, all of them are regarded as belonging to a more secular or "social" category than the dances so far listed:

jä:hko:wa:ʔ ʔoɛnɔʔ 'Pigeon Dance'

joʔä:kaʔ ʔoɛnɔʔ 'Raccoon Dance'

kɛjɔh ʔoɛnɔʔ 'Fish Dance'

kɛɔtanέhkwih ʔoɛnɔʔ 'Horse Dance' ('Had-a-Horse' WNF)

kwaʔyɔ:ʔ ʔoɛnɔʔ 'Rabbit Dance'

so:wäk ʔoɛnɔʔ 'Duck Dance'

takä:ʔɛ:ʔ ʔoɛnɔʔ 'Chicken Dance'

tekáʔnɔ:tɔ:t ʔoɛnɔʔ 'Alligator Dance'

thwɛ:t or thwaɛt ʔoɛnɔʔ 'Swan Dance'

tyɔ́:yaik ʔoɛnɔʔ 'Robin Dance'

kaksokɛ:yɔ:ʔ [*guk-sa'-gä-ne-a*—LHM] 'Grinding Dishes'

kanestɔkä:ʔe:ʔ 'Beating the Dry Skin'

kashéʔtɔta:ʔtɔh 'Shaking the Jug'

kaskoɛɔ́taʔtɔh [*os-ko-dä'-tä*—LHM] 'Shaking the Bush'

kaʔnóstaʔke:khaːʔ 'Naked Dance,' literally 'characterized by nakedness' (identical with the preceding)

kayó:waka:yɔh 'Old Moccasin'

tewatsihásyɔʔɔ:ʔ 'Garter Dance'

waʔέnothi:yɔʔ 'Sharpening the Stick'

tyɔtatenyátkä:s 'Grab Your Partner' (RE), 'Choose a Partner' (WNF), literally 'they grab each other'

yɔtatyaʔtasyɔnyáʔthaʔ 'Preparation Dance' (LHM), literally 'they prepare themselves with it'

ʔonέshɛʔtɔh 'Arm-Shaking Dance' (LHM), literally 'dropped arm'

ʔoshé:wɛʔ 'Falling Belly'
ʔoyataʔké:aʔ 'Cherokee Stomp Dance' ('Stomp Dance, Snake
Dance'—RE), literally 'cave people, Cherokee'

F. Games and Associated Terminology

A general word for game is kayɛ:taʔ. ta:tiyέɔʔ means 'they
are playing, betting'; tá:yɛɔʔ 'he's playing'; teyéyɛɔʔ 'she's playing.'

Names for the Bowl Game were given on p. 31. Terms for win-
ning throws in this game are:

ʔo:ɛtaʔ (all six stones identical; wins five bean counters), literally 'planted field'; ʔoʔkáɛta:ɛʔ 'it came up with all six identical'

ʔonyo:ʔah (all identical but one; wins one bean), literally 'almost
wild'

Other terminology relating to the Bowl Game includes:

yesáeʔtä:kwas 'she picks out the beans' ('bean watcher'—WNF)
yeka:nyaʔs 'she pays' ('payer'—WNF)
honɔ́tkaɛɔʔ 'they're watching' ('referees'—WNF)
honɔ́steistɔh (identical with the preceding), literally 'they're
managing it'
hí:es 'they (two) collect (the bets)'
(ʔo)tísaskɔk 'skunking' (loss of one's turn without having won
a single bean)

A similar game is kaskɛʔisé:htɔh [*gus-ga-e-sa'-tä*—LHM]
'Deer Buttons' (LHM), 'Buttons, Indian Dice' (RE). The win-
ning throws in this game are:

ʔo:ɛtaʔ (all eight dice identical; wins twenty beans if two are
playing, five if more than two)

ʔo:nyɔ́hsaʔ (all identical but one; wins four beans if two are
playing, two if more than two), literally 'squash'

ʔonyo:ʔah (all identical but two; wins two beans if two are playing, one if more than two)

If a player has been eliminated but is able to pay his debt to
the winner, he is told tekhni:ʔɛhséji:wɛt 'you will have two free
throws,' literally 'you will hammer twice.' If he is not able to pay
his debt, he is told ska:t ʔɛhséji:wɛt 'you will hammer once.'

The Snowsnake game, as well as the snowsnake itself, is called
ka:wa:saʔ [*ga-wa'-sa*—LHM]. Parts of the snowsnake are:
katkwíäʔkeh 'tail'

kakóta?keh 'nose' ('head'—ACP)
ka:néko:a? 'lead on the end'

Other associated terms include:

ka?owɔkɔ:h 'trough' ('track'—RE)
hatiyɛhtáhkwa? 'mouth of the trough' (ACP), literally 'where
they strike'
he:otye?s 'he throws, thrower'
ye:wásohka:tha? 'snowsnake medicine (wax),' literally 'they
use it to make the snowsnake slippery'
swa:kam (identical with the preceding; regarded by some as an
English word)

The Hoop and Javelin game is called either kake:ta? [gä-geh'-
dä—LHM] or, less commonly kanó?ka?o:?. Associated terms
are:

ka?hnya? 'stick' ('javelin')
kanó?kä:? 'hoop' (also 'poplar')
?ɛ?níka:a? 'hoop' (another name)

Other Seneca games include:

té:nɔ?ɛni:ya:s 'Tug-of-War,' literally 'they pull the pole'
tewá?ä:ɔ? 'Lacrosse, lacrosse stick,' literally 'net on it'
yé:hsɛthwas 'Football,' literally 'they kick'
tɛ:né:hta:s 'Foot Race,' literally 'they run'
tɛ:nɔtatye:nɔ:s 'Westling,' literally 'they grab each other'
tɛ:nɔhtahkwayéɔ? 'Moccasin Game,' literally 'they bet on a shoe'

G. Terminology of the Iroquois League

The Condolence Ceremony is called ?atyä:khɔ́sha?ko:wa:h,
literally 'the great feast.' Related terms include:

ka?nikɔ́ɛkeskwɛh 'condolence, consolation,' literally 'the mind is
raised'
kajístayɛ? 'council fire,' literally 'the fire is there'
jokté:sko:wa:h 'the great long roots'
?onähtají?ko:wa:h 'the great black leaves'

The "four cardinal principles of Iroquois policy" (WNF) are:

skɛ:nɔ? 'health, peace'
ka?hásteshä? 'strength, civil authority'
káiwi:yo:h 'truth, righteousness'
kayaneshä?ko:wa:h 'the great law, the commonwealth'

Characters in the Deganawida legend include:

tekanɔwi:tah 'Deganawida'
hayɔ́:wɛ:thaʔ 'Hiawatha'
thatota:hoʔ 'Tadodaho'
jikɔ́hsahsɛʔ 'the Peace Queen,' also 'wildcat,' literally 'fat face'

3. Classifications of Nature

A. Numerals

The numerals from one to ten are:

ska:t 'one'	**ye:iʔ** 'six'
tekhni:h 'two'	**ja:tak** 'seven'
sɛh 'three'	**tekyɔʔ** 'eight'
ke:ih 'four'	**tyohtɔ:h** 'nine'
wis 'five'	**washɛ:h** 'ten'

The numerals eleven through nineteen are formed with the addition of **ska:eʔ**, as follows:

ská: ska:eʔ 'eleven'
tekhní: ska:eʔ 'twelve'
sɛ́ ska:eʔ 'thirteen'

The formation of numerals above nineteen is illustrated below:

tewáshɛ:h 'twenty'
tewáshɛ: ská: ska:eʔ or **tewáshɛ: ska:t** 'twenty-one'
sɛ niwáshɛ:h 'thirty'
ke:i niwáshɛ:h 'forty'
ska:t tewɛ́ʔnyaʔe:h 'one hundred,' literally 'one strike of the hand'
ska:t nɔʔtewɛʔnyaʔeshäshɛ:h 'one thousand,' literally 'ten hundreds'

B. Measurements

Time

The hours of the day are referred to as follows:

ska:t jóistaʔe:h 'one o'clock,' literally 'one strike'
tekhni: teyóista:ʔe:h 'two o'clock'
sɛ niyóista:ʔe:h 'three o'clock'
ke:i niyóista:ʔe:h 'four o'clock' (etc.)

References to parts of the day are:

ʔɛ:teh 'day, daytime'
teyóhatheh 'it is light'
tawɛtɔ:tiʔ 'daybreak,' literally 'the day opens'
tyohɛ́ʔɔh 'daybreak,' literally 'it has dawned'
tawɛ́ʔnyaka:eʔ 'daybreak,' literally 'the hand makes a noise'
setéhjiah 'early in the morning'
wɛ:nishäséʔa:neh 'morning, forenoon,' literally 'early in the day'
haʔtewɛ:níshɛ:h 'noon, midday'
hekã:hkwa:ʔah 'afternoon,' literally 'less sun'
wɛta:jis 'evening,' literally 'the day darkens'
ʔoʔkã:sʔah 'evening,' literally 'partly night'
waʔóʔkä:h 'night'
sɔeh 'night, nighttime'
haʔtéwahsɔ:thwɛh 'midnight'
ʔotɛ́:nisyoʔk 'the end of the day'

Related terms are:

the:tɛʔ 'yesterday'
wɛ:nishäteʔ 'today'
wahsɔtateʔ 'tonight'
ʔɛyo:hɛʔt 'tomorrow'
waʔo:hɛʔt 'the next day'
ska:t ʔɛyo:ta:ʔ 'one day from now'
tekhni: tɛyo:ta:ʔ 'two days from now'
sɛ nɛyo:ta:ʔ 'three days from now'

There are several ways of referring to the days of the week. A
set of names used on the Cattaraugus Reservation is:

ʔawɛtatókɛhtɔh 'Sunday'
ʔoʔwɛtɛ:taʔt 'Monday'
swɛta:tih 'Tuesday' or 'any day after Monday'
haʔtewɛtáɛh 'Wednesday'
haʔtewɛtáɛ ʔɛyóhɛʔtkeh 'Thursday'
wis watɔ:thaʔ wɛ:nishäteʔ 'Friday,' sometimes 'Thursday'
wɛ:ta:k 'Saturday'

On the Tonawanda Reservation the days are simply counted,
starting with Monday:

ska:t wɛ:nishæteʔ 'day number one, Monday'
tekhni: wɛ:nishæteʔ 'Tuesday' (etc.)

There is a similar usage on the Allegany Reservation, but

wɛ:nishätéhkɔh may be substituted for wɛ:níshäteʔ. Other names sometimes heard are:

teyotɛ:nitsiyáʔkɔh 'Sunday,' literally 'the broken day'
wɛta:kʔah 'Friday,' literally 'almost Saturday'
niyenɔktówaes 'Saturday,' literally 'when they wash the room'

There are 12 month or moon names. During the winter, one of them usually does service for two successive moons to make the year come out even. The first moon is correlated with the position of the Pleiades. A list obtained on the Cattaraugus Reservation is:

1. niskówakhneh or niskáwakhneh
2. niyoʔnotʔá:h 'the frogs are almost peeping'
3. ʔoʔnótʔah 'the frogs are peeping'
4. kanɔ́ʔkat (referring to hills for corn?)
5. ʔoyáikhneh or yáikhneh (referring to the ripening of berries?)
6. skáiskekhneh or háiskekhneh
7. skayɛ́:neah or hayɛ́:neah
8. kɛtɛ́ʔɔkhneh
9. kɛ́:ɔkhneh
10. kahsáʔkhneh 'when I cough'
11. jotho:h 'when it is cold'
12. nisʔah

Another list, from the Allegany Reservation, adds wéɔtahkwaʔ 'when the blossoms are on' after kanɔ́ʔkat and omits jotho:h. Other names are:

wá:kaita:thɔh 'the road slopes this way and that' (as the sun melts the snow)
kanähtokʔah 'the end of the leaves'

Words for phases of the moon are:

kaʔéhta:ʔ 'new moon,' literally 'fingernail in (the sky)'
wɛ:níʔtase:ʔ 'new moon' (also sawátähkwa:ɛʔ 'the moon gets on it again')
haʔtewɛ:níʔtaɛh 'middle of the moon'
watɛ:niʔtóʔkthaʔ 'end of the moon'

Words for seasons are:

kɛkwítekhneh 'spring'
kɛhé:neh or kakɛ́hɔteʔ 'summer'
koshé:neh or yoshä:teʔ 'winter' (the latter also 'year')

Length

The following words are used in measuring length:

(ska:t) joyɔ́hkä:t '1 inch,' literally 'one thumb'
(tekhni:) teyóyɔhkä:ke:h '2 inches'
sɛ niyóyɔhkä:ke:h '3 inches' (etc.)
(ska:t) joʔɛ:no:t '1 yard,' literally 'one pole'
(tekhni:) teyóʔɛnɔ:ke:h '2 yards'
sɛ niyóʔɛnɔ:ke:h '3 yards' (etc.)
(ska:t) jóaʔa:t '1 rod, pace'
(tekhni:) teyóaʔa:ke:h '2 paces'
sɛ niyóaʔa:ke:h '3 paces' (etc.)
ska:t heyótkathwɛh '1 mile,' literally 'as far as can be seen'
tekhni: heyótkathwɛh '2 miles' (etc.)

Volume

Some measures of volume are:

kanɔ:tsi:h 'quart,' literally 'small basketful'
skaʔa:tsi:h 'bushel,' literally 'basketful'

C. Colors

Two verb stems that may be used to refer to specific colors are -kɛ:ɛt 'be light-colored, white' and -aji:h 'be dark-colored, black':

kakɛ:ɛt 'it is white'
kanóhsakɛ:ɛt 'white house'
wa:ji:h 'it is black'
ʔóäʔtaji:h 'black feather'

A number of other words contain the stem -ʔɛ:ʔ 'be the color of':

tkwɛ́htä:ʔɛ:ʔ 'red' (origin uncertain)
ʔoʔshéäʔɛ:ʔ 'purple, the color of scoke'
jítkwä:ʔɛ:ʔ 'yellow, the color of bile'
jɛ:stáʔɛ:ʔ 'black, the color of charcoal'
ʔoʔkɛ́:ʔɛ:ʔ 'gray, the color of ashes'
ʔoiskwanyɛ́ʔtaʔɛ:ʔ 'brown, the color of rotten wood'

Other words used to express color are kanähtaikhɔʔ 'green' and ji:nyóaeʔ 'blue.'

Shades may be indicated by one of the two stems mentioned first above: ʔotkwɛ́htä:ji:h 'dark red.' Approximation to a color may be shown by the diminutive suffix: ʔoʔkɛ́:ʔɛ:ʔɔh 'grayish.'

D. Biological Terms

Plants and Animals

Both plants and animals may be classified as either **kanyo:ˀ** 'wild' or **kashe:nɛˀ** 'cultivated, domestic.'

Roughly according to its size, a wild plant may be one of the following:

ˀoˀéohtaˀ 'weed, herb'
ˀoyɔ:wɔˀ 'tall weed'
ˀoskawayɛˀ 'bush'
kä:it or **ka:ɔtaˀ** 'tree'

A grove is **kaha:to:t** and a forest **kaha:taˀ**. Further names for animals and plants will be found in 2C (p. 32), 2E (p. 34), and especially 4G (p. 49).

Body Parts

The following are the names of some body parts:

ˀonɔ́ˀɛ:ˀ 'head'
ˀakékeˀä? 'my hair'
kekɛ́ˀjaˀkeh '(on) my forehead'
kekáːˀkeh '(on) my eyes'
ˀokahkwéohsaˀ 'eyebrows'
kekɔ́taˀkeh '(on) my nose'
káɔhtaˀ 'my ear'
katahoskwáˀkeh '(on) my cheeks'
kehsáka:ɛt 'my mouth'
keskwãːˀkeh '(on) my lips'
ˀonɔ́ˀjaˀ 'tooth'
kaˀnɔ́hsaˀkeh '(on) my tongue'
kyoˀháˀkeh '(on) my chin, jaw'
ke:nyáˀsaˀkeh '(on) my neck, throat'
kenyãːˀkeh '(on) my neck, collar'
khnɛhsáˀkeh '(on) my shoulder'
khnɛshaˀ 'my arm'
khyostäːˀkeh '(on) my elbow'
khnɛshóˀkwaˀ 'my wrist'
kesˀóhtaˀ 'my hand'
käkwáhtaˀkeh '(on) my palm, sole'
keˀnyaˀ 'my finger'
kyɔhkãːˀkeh '(on) my thumb'
ˀakéˀehtaˀ 'my fingernail'
keˀtɔ́hsäˀkeh '(on) my chest'

keswéʔnɔʔkeh '(on) my back'
keswaʔ 'my rib cage'
ʔakhnɔ́ʔkwaʔkeh '(on) my breasts, lungs'
ʔoshé:waʔ 'belly'
ʔotkwístaʔ 'stomach'
ʔoksɔ:wɛʔ 'intestines'
ʔakéthwɛhsaʔ 'my liver'
ʔokáhkweʔnɔʔ 'kidney'
kanäʔ 'penis'
ʔoyáhkɛʔtaʔ 'head of the penis'
keʔhɔ́hsaʔkeh '(on) my testicles'
ka:nɛ:ɛʔ 'vagina'
ʔo:nɔ́ʔshaʔ 'buttocks'
ʔoʔyáka:ɛt 'anus'
kejiskoʔkwáʔkeh '(on) my hip'
kahsi:nɔʔ 'leg'
kyahtáʔkeh '(on) my thigh'
kɔsháʔkeh '(on) my knee'
kejioʔkwáʔkeh '(on) my ankle'
kahsíʔtaʔ 'my foot'
khyakwi:yäʔ 'my toe'

E. Cosmographic Terms

Geological Features

yɔɛjateʔ 'the earth, land'
ʔonɔ:taʔ 'hill'
yoäkɔ:h 'valley, bottom land'
ʔóehtaʔ 'soil'
ʔoʔnéhsaʔ 'sand'
kaʔskwa:aʔ 'stone'
kastɛ́:teʔ 'cliff, rock bank'
kɛhɔ:teʔ 'river, stream'
kanyotaeʔ 'lake'
kanyoteowanɛh 'ocean,' literally 'big lake'

Points of the Compass

ʔothóweʔkeh 'north,' literally 'where it is cold'
tkä:hkwitkɛʔs 'east,' literally 'where the sun rises'
ʔonénɔʔkeh 'south,' literally 'where it is warm'; also ʔɛtyék-kwa:h
    or ʔɔtyék-kwa:h
hekä:hkwɛʔs 'west,' literally 'where the sun sets'

Meteorological Phenomena

kä:ha? 'the wind is blowing'
?ohjí?ke? 'it's cloudy'
?ostɛɔtyɔ:h 'it's raining'
?osta:a? 'rain'
?o?kyɔ:tyɔ:h 'it's snowing'
?o?kä? 'snow' (in the air)
?oni:ya? 'snow' (on the ground)
?o?néyostɔ:tyɔ:h 'it's hailing'
?o?néyosta? 'hail' (also 'hominy grains')
?owisyɔtyɔ:h 'it's sleeting'
?owi:sä? 'ice' (also 'butter')
kashatɔtye?s 'it's misting'
?osha:ta? 'mist, fog'
?o?twɛniho? 'lightning flashed'
?o?káyɛ?kyɔ:? 'lightning struck'
hatiwɛnotatye?s 'thunder'
?o?ha:ot 'rainbow'
?o?twátyɔ:yatyɛɔnyɔ:? 'aurora borealis,' literally 'the sky became abnormal'

Astronomical Phenomena

Both the sun and the moon are referred to with the one word kä:hkwa:?, literally 'the sun or moon is in it' (that is, in the sky). Which of the two is meant can be specified by preceding the above word with ?ɛte:kha:? 'diurnal' or sɔekha:? 'nocturnal.' Names for phases of the moon can be found on p. 39. An eclipse is called ?ɛkä:hkwáhtɔ?t 'the sun or moon will disappear.' A star is ?ojíhsɔ?ta?. Names of particular stars and constellations are:

kɛtéɔwi:tha? 'morning star,' literally 'it leads the meadow'
nyakwai? tethakɔswá?ha:? 'north star' [?], literally 'bear sticking his nose out'
nyakwai? hatíshe? 'Ursa Major,' literally 'they're chasing a bear'
hatítkwa?ta:? 'the Pleiades'

4. Material Culture

A. Ceremonial Equipment

Musical Instruments

A general word for an instrument that is used to accompany

singing is yɔtɛnotáhkwaʔ 'people use it to sing with.'
yɔtɛnotahkwaʔshɔ́ʔɔh (HCC) is specifically plural.

Rattles. The general word for rattle is kastáwɛʔsäʔ or
kastɔ́wɛʔsäʔ. It may be qualified in various, not entirely standardized ways to specify a particular type of rattle:

ʔonɔ́ʔkä:ʔ kastáwɛʔsäʔ 'horn rattle'
ʔosnɔʔ kastáwɛʔsäʔ 'bark rattle'
ʔo:nyáʔsaʔ kastáwɛʔsäʔ 'squash or gourd rattle'
ʔo:nyɔ́hsaʔ kastáwɛʔsäʔ (identical with the preceding)
yí:ʔtosthaʔ kastáwɛʔsäʔ (also identical with the two preceding)
káistatkos kastáwɛʔsäʔ 'tin rattle'
ʔo:nyóʔkwaʔ kastáwɛʔsäʔ 'nut rattle' (HCC, p. 287, referring to
a coconut rattle)

A rattle made from a turtle is called kaʔno:waʔ. This word may
be qualified as:

kanyáhtɛ:h kaʔno:waʔ 'snapping turtle rattle' ('great turtle
rattle'—HCC)
kaʔtya:skwaʔ or kaʔja:skwaʔ kaʔno:waʔ 'box turtle rattle'
yɔthɔwisáthaʔ kaʔno:waʔ (identical with the preceding)

Drums. There are two names in common use for the 'water
drum' ('drum, tom-tom'—RE):

kaʔnɔ́hko:ɔh, literally 'covered keg'
kanɔ́ʔjo:ɔh [gä-no-jo'-o—LHM], literally 'covered bucket'

There is no separate designation for the somewhat larger
drum ('big water drum'—HCC) used in the ʔohki:we:h ceremony (p. 33), but it may be distinguished by the addition of
ʔohki:we: before one of the above words. A drumstick is called
yeʔnɔhkwaʔésthaʔ, literally 'people use it for striking the keg.'

Other musical instruments include:

kaʔhnyaʔ 'stick, club' ('stamping stick, tempo beater'—HCC)
kaʔwástaʔ 'stick' (identical with the preceding)
ʔatáʔtishäʔ 'cane'
ka:nóʔskä:ʔ 'notches' ('rasping sticks'—HCC)
kashéwɛʔtaʔ 'bells, sleigh bells'
ká:ʔkɛ:taʔ 'flute' ('Indian flute'—HCC)
ye:oʔtáwasthaʔ 'flute' ('white man's flute'—HCC)
yéɔʔtasthaʔ 'flute,' literally 'people use it for blowing'

Other Ceremonial Equipment

kakɔ́hsaʔ 'false-face'

kajíhsaʔ 'husk-face'

ʔoyέʔkwaʔ 'tobacco'

ʔoyέʔkwaʔɔ:weh 'Indian tobacco' (*Nicotiana rustica*)

ʔoyε:έʔ 'bead, wampum'

ʔotkóäʔ or ʔotkóʔäʔ 'wampum string'

kaswέhtaʔ 'wampum belt'

kaji:staʔ 'wampum,' literally 'ember, light'

kajístakwɛni:yoʔ 'the main wampum,' specifically that kept at Tonawanda to validate the Handsome Lake religion

kanɛshatiyɔtáhkwaʔ 'tally stick' with attached wampum ('invitation wampum'—RE), literally 'used for extending the arm'

ka:nóʔskeotɔʔ (identical with the preceding), literally 'notches on it'

kané ʔäʔ 'Eagle Dance fan, feather stick'

ka:yáʔehtaʔ 'Eagle Dance pole'

yeneʔkwä:ʔesthaʔ kaʔhnyaʔ 'Eagle Dance striking stick'

kanɔ́hse:s 'longhouse' (kanɔ́hseskeh 'at the longhouse')

yekhɔ́nyaʔthaʔ 'cookhouse,' literally 'they use it for making food'

kajíʔka:ye:s 'bench,' literally 'long chair'

B. Clothing and Costume Components

ʔasyɔ́nyashäʔ 'clothing'

ʔoswa:tɛ:h 'woman's costume'

kɛhikwa:aʔ 'hat'

wáɔshaʔ 'cap'

kasto:wäʔ [*gus-to'-weh*—LHM] 'headdress'

kayahtowéʔshäʔ 'pants'

kaʔkha:aʔ [*gä-ka'-ah*—LHM] 'skirt'

káishäʔ [*gise'-ha*—LHM] 'leggings'

ʔatyaʔtawíʔshäʔ [*ah-de-a-dä-we-sä*—LHM] 'overdress, smock'

ka:wáhashäʔ 'belt' (worn around waist)

teyɔthwahásthaʔ (identical with the preceding)

kakéhtaʔ [*gä-geh'-tä*—LHM] 'belt' (worn over shoulder and around waist)

ʔatotä:ʔ 'shoulder belt, suspenders'

kakéʔtaʔ (worn on upper part of leg, with high boots attached to it)

tewatsihásyɔʔɔ:ʔ 'garters'

kayó:wah 'moccasin'

ʔahtáhkwaʔ 'shoe'

ʔahtáhkwaʔɔ:weh [ah-tä-quä-o'-weh—LHM] 'native shoe, moccasin'

yɛnɛshahásthaʔ [yeu-nis-hä-hos-ta—LHM] 'arm band'

yɛnɛshoʔkwáhasthaʔ [yen-nis-ho-quä-hos-tä — LHM] 'wrist band'

yɔtsinɔhɔ́sthaʔ [yen-che-no-hos-ta-tä—LHM] 'leg band'

ʔotsinonɔ́hkä:ʔ (identical with the preceding)

ʔaʔwáshä:ʔ [ah-was-ha—LHM] 'earring'

ʔɛʔnyáhashä? [ah-ne-a-hus-ha—LHM] 'finger ring'

yɛníhtyasthaʔ 'necklace'

yɔthwistaniyɔtáhkwaʔ [out-wis-tä-ne-un-dä-quä—LHM] 'silver beads, pendants'

ʔɛ:nyáskä:ʔ [an-ne-äs-ga—LHM] 'brooch'

ʔoʔówaʔah (a brooch shape), literally 'like an owl'

teyóɛwɛ:ke:h (another brooch shape), literally 'two wires'

C. Basketry

Materials and Components

kanyɔh 'white ash' (*Fraxinus americana*)

yɛɔtakwæ:sɔs 'black ash' (*Fraxinus nigra*)

kaká?taʔ 'white oak' (*Quercus alba*)

kɔ́hso:ʔ 'red maple, soft maple' (*Acer rubrum*)

ʔonɔnoka:aʔ 'hickory' (*Carya ovata*)

jistakɛ́:ɛʔ (identical with the preceding)

jokä:ka:s (identical with the two preceding)

ʔo:wɛ́ʔkä:ʔ 'splint, wood as a material'

ʔohsóhkwaʔ 'paint, dye'

kɛ?tɔ:wɛʔ 'bottom, base'

tekɛʔtowɛ́ʔse:ʔ 'double bottom'

yɔthwatasétha? literally 'people use it to go around' ('flexible withe, weft element'—ML)

teyɔʔɛnɔ́:hkwaʔ literally 'people use it for putting the stick on' ('inner rim splint'—ML)

ʔaste:kha:ʔ 'outer part' ('outer rim splint'—ML)

ʔoʔnowɛɔnyɔʔ 'flat curls,' literally 'bugs (?) in it'

ʔojíʔsyɔyo:tɔʔ 'peaked curls,' literally 'standing curls'

Techniques

yɔ:wɛ́ʔkɛ:ɔnih 'they are making splints'

ye:wɛʔkä:tokɛ́stha? 'they are straightening out the splints' ('trimming'—ML)

yɔ:wɛʔkä:ke:tas 'they are scraping the splints'
tɛhsataʔɛnɔɛʔ 'you will hem the top,' literally 'put on the stick'
tɛwaʔɛnɔ́:ɔk 'it will be hemmed'

Types

kaʔáshäʔ [gase-ha—LHM] 'basket'
yä:hkwaʔ 'container'
yɔtɛnɔʔshä:hkwaʔ 'food basket'
yeʔnístä:hkwaʔ 'corn basket'
yenonɔʔtä:hkwaʔ 'potato basket'
yestakwä:tahkwaʔ 'dirty clothes basket, hamper'
yenɔ́htä:hkwaʔ 'comb basket'
yeʔnikhɔshä:hkwaʔ 'sewing basket'
yɔtkéhtasthaʔ 'pack basket'
yeʔnistanɛ́hkwisthaʔ, literally 'they use it for bringing in the
  corn'
yɔtasheʔnɔ́tahkwaʔ 'basket attached at the waist for planting or
  berry picking,' literally 'they put a lump on them'
yekaehtowä̃:ʔthaʔ 'corn washing basket, hulling basket'
yɛwɔ:kthaʔ 'sifter, sieve'
yoʔkɛ́:wɔ:kthaʔ 'ash sifter'
ʔoʔnɛ́yostowanɛs 'hominy sifter,' literally 'big grains'
ʔonɔ:shäʔ 'small corn husk basket'
kashéʔtaʔ [gos-ha'-dä—LHM] 'bottle, jug'
yejikheʔtä:hkwaʔ 'salt container, salt bottle'
watáshaenɛʔs 'drop handle basket'
tekaʔashä:ɔh 'cross basket'

Other Basketry Terms

kasha:aʔ 'halter, strap, burden strap'
kanɔ́hsɔta:aʔ (identical with the preceding)
yeʔásyohka:thaʔ 'basket medicine, agrimony' (Agrimonia gry-
  posepala), literally 'they sprinkle baskets with it'
haʔno:waʔ óishäʔ 'pitcher plant' (Sarracenia purpurea),
  literally 'turtle's leggings' (trapped water used as basket
  medicine)

D. Agricultural and Cooking Implements

ʔato:kɛʔ 'ax' (cf. ʔaʔskwíhsaʔ p. 48)
ye:htakahathwáthaʔ 'plow,' literally 'they use it to turn over
  the soil'
yakókwathaʔ 'digging tool'

káɔhjishä^ɔ 'hoe'

yeyέthwatha^ɔ 'planting tool'

yetáhkwa^ɔ '(corn) crib,' literally 'they put things in it'

yenowiyá^ɔktha^ɔ 'husking pin'

ka^ɔnékahta^ɔ [*gä-ne'-gä-ta*—LHM] 'mortar'

hetkɛ:kha:^ɔ 'pestle,' literally 'upper part'

yethé^ɔtahkwa^ɔ (identical with the preceding), literally 'they use
　　it for pounding'

yɔteka^ɔtáhkwa^ɔ 'fire-making tool'

^ɔoksa^ɔ 'dish'

kajɛ^ɔ [*ga-jih*—LHM] 'bowl'

ka:ɔwɔ^ɔ 'tray' (also 'boat')

kanɔ́^ɔja^ɔ 'kettle, pot'

kanɔ́^ɔjowa:nɛh 'big kettle'

kanɔ́^ɔja^ɔɔ:weh 'old-fashioned Indian kettle'

yeshe^ɔɔnyá^ɔtha^ɔ 'dough-making bowl'

^ɔatókwa^ɔshä^ɔ 'spoon, ladle'

^ɔatókwa^ɔsyowanɛh 'big spoon'

katkónya^ɔshä^ɔ [*got'-go-ne-os-ha'*—LHM] 'ladle, paddle, stirring
　　implement'

yetkónya^ɔtha^ɔ (identical with the preceding)

katkónya^ɔsyowanɛh 'big ladle'

nikatkonya^ɔshæ^ɔá:h 'small ladle'

kahsikwä:^ɔ 'fork'

kakánya^ɔshä^ɔ 'knife'

E. Weapons

^ɔa^ɔskwíhsa^ɔ 'ax, tomahawk'

^ɔo^ɔskwíhsɔ:t [*o-sque'-sont*—LHM; identical with the preceding]

kají:wa^ɔ [*gä-je'-wä*—LHM] 'hammer, war club'

kanɔ^ɔkéotashä^ɔ [*ga-ne-u'-ga-o-dus-ha*—LHM] 'horn war club'

ka^ɔnɔ^ɔ [*gä'-no*—LHM] 'arrow'

wa^ɔɛ:nɔ^ɔ [*wä-a'-no*—LHM] 'bow' (also 'pole, stick')

ka^ɔta:shä^ɔ [*gä-däs-ha*—LHM] 'quiver, sheaf'

F. Other Artifacts

kɛ:wɛ:^ɔ 'wire, needle, nail'

tewatyawɛɔkótha^ɔ 'needle'

ye:wɛ́:tahkwa^ɔ [*ya-wa-o-dä-quä*—LHM] 'needle book'

yɛ:wéotahkwa^ɔ [*yä-wä-o-dä-quä*—LHM] 'pincushion'

ʔojɔ́tkä:ʔ 'hook, hanger'
kastɔ́ʔshäʔ 'fishhook'
yɔʔkáhtahkwaʔ 'punch'
teyɔʔistáhkwaʔ 'drill'
teyekɛsyɔ́ʔthaʔ 'scraper'
yɔhkeokwáthaʔ [*uh'-ga-o-gwät'-hä*—LHM] 'chisel,' literally
 'they use it to scatter chips'
yɔtkétathaʔ '(back) scratcher'
yejistɔtáhkwaʔ 'lamp'
teyestä:theʔtáhkwaʔ 'polish'
kayáʔtaʔ 'doll'
ʔashókwahtaʔ [*ah-so-quä'-tä*—LHM] 'pipe'
teye:wɛʔkeotáhkwaʔ 'snowshoe, ski,' literally 'they use the wood
 for standing upright'
yɛʔnikɔhsákehta:sthaʔ 'frame for carrying a large object on
 one's back'
ʔatätahkwaʔ [*ah-dä'-dä-quä*—LHM] 'saddle,' literally 'used for
 getting on'
ʔatyáʔtota:aʔ (identical with the preceding), literally 'it's put
 over its body'
yɔke:shäʔ or yɔkɛ:shäʔ [*yun-ga'-sa*—LHM] 'pocket'
katkwɛ́ʔtaʔ [*got-kwen-dä*—LHM] 'pocketbook'
yeyɛ́ʔkwata:hkwaʔ 'tobacco pouch'
káɔhkä:ʔ 'rope'
ka:wáhashäʔ [*gä-swä-hos-hä* [?]—LHM] 'band'
kajíhsaʔ 'husk mat' (also 'husk-face'; cf. p. 45)
kɛska:aʔ 'sleeping mat'
yɔtyä:tɛhtä:hkwaʔ 'mattress,' literally 'bag for laying out flat'
ʔi:yo:s 'blanket'
ka:nyáʔkhaɔʔ 'quilt,' literally 'put together piece by piece'
kakɔ́ʔsäʔ 'pillow'
ka:ɔyɔ:t 'swing, hammock, cradle,' literally 'attached boat'
kaɔwɔni:yɔ:t (identical with the preceding), literally 'hanging
 boat'
ka:ɔwɔ́ʔ 'boat' (also 'tray'; cf. p. 48)

G. Foods

The following are general terms referring to food:
kakhwaʔ 'food'
tyɔhéhkɔh [*de-o-ha'-ko*—LHM] 'our sustenance, our life sup-
 porters' ('the vegetables'—RE), literally 'what we live on'
 (referring to corn, beans, and squash)

Corn (Zea mays)

The generic word for corn is ʔonέɔʔ, which may also refer to the kernel. Other parts of the corn plant are:

ʔoeä? 'cornstalk'
ʔojíʔjo:t 'tassle,' literally 'standing tassle'
ʔojíʔjo:aʔ (identical with the preceding), literally 'tassle on the end'
ʔokyo:t 'corn silk' (protruding from husk)
ʔokäʔäh 'corn silk' (inside husk)
ʔojówɔhsaʔ 'corn leaf'
ʔo:wέʔtaʔ 'ear with husk'
ʔoʔnístaʔ 'ear without husk but with kernels'
ʔonóhkwaʔɛʔ or ʔonóhkwɛʔɛʔ 'ear without kernels, corncob'
ʔono:nyaʔ 'husk'
ʔo:ateʔ 'row of kernels' (also 'road')
ʔokójiʔtaʔ 'corn pollen' (ACP)
ʔokáehtaʔ 'hull'

The following varieties of corn are named (botanical classifications are from ACP) :

ʔonέɔkɛ:ɛt [o-na-o'-ga-ant—LHM] 'white corn' ('Tuscarora or squaw corn'—ACP; *Zea mays amylacea* 'soft corn')
héhko:wa:h [*ha-go'-wä*—LHM] 'calico or hominy corn' (*Zea mays indurata* 'flint corn')
ʔonɛ:hsáhkwaʔ or ʔonɛ:hsóhkwaʔ 'popcorn' (*Zea mays everta*)
wahtatɔkwas (identical with the preceding), literally 'it bursts'
ʔonέɔʔɔ:weh 'old-fashioned or native corn' ('sacred corn'—ACP; *Zea mays tunicata* 'pod corn')
ʔonέɔjiʔ 'black or dark corn' (variety uncertain)

Aside from specific food preparations, corn may be found in the following conditions:

ʔosäʔah 'green corn'
ʔoji:kwɛs 'corn smut' (also 'venereal disease')
ʔotkiʔ onέɔʔ 'foul or decayed corn'
ʔonέɔkwe:kɔh 'whole corn'
ʔoʔnέyostaʔ 'cracked corn, hominy grains'
ʔostέʔsäʔ 'braided corn'

The following terms are related to the growing and initial preparation of corn:

kanέ:ɔkwɛʔ 'seed corn'

ʔostísta:neʔ (*Hystrix patula*) (FWW), a corn medicine, 'bottle-brush grass'

kahsáʔkɛ:taʔ (*Phragmites communis*) (FWW), another corn medicine, 'common reed'

hatiʔnisté:es 'they are gathering, picking corn'

hatinowi:yaʔs 'they are husking corn'

hatinɔnyɔ:thaʔ 'they are pulling back the husk' (for braiding)

ʔonɔ:nyɔ:t 'the husk is pulled back'

hatístɛʔsyɔ:nih 'they are braiding corn'

hatikáehtawa:s 'they are winnowing it,' literally 'sifting the hulls'

Corn preparations have the following names:

ʔonó:hkwaʔ '(hulled) corn soup'

ʔonɛ́:ʔtaʔ 'burnt or roasted corn soup'

ʔokɔ:säʔ 'baked corn'

ʔokɔsäkiʔ 'baked corn soup'

kakɔsäkí:ʔta:ʔ 'fried baked corn'

ʔoʔnéyosta:kiʔ 'cracked corn soup' ('corn soup liquor, samp'— ACP)

ʔoshɔwɛ:ʔ 'corn pudding' (ACP), 'parched corn' (MRH), 'false-face mush' (RE)

ʔojískwaʔ or ʔoji:skwaʔ 'mush, pudding'

ʔoshɔwɛ:ʔ ʔojískwaʔ 'parched corn mush' (MRH)

kakɔ́hsaʔ ʔojískwaʔ 'false-face mush' (cf. ʔoshɔwɛ:ʔ)

kajískwaʔe:ʔ ʔojískwaʔ 'ball players' mush'

ʔonɔtä:ʔ 'hominy'

ʔohɔ́:staʔ 'dumpling'

ʔoʔnistakáʔɔh 'good tasting corn' ('boiled green corn'—ACP)

ʔonɔ́ʔkhwishäʔ 'boiled and sweetened corn'

ʔonyáhjiʔtaʔ 'corn cooked in husk, tamale'

kaʔnístɛʔta:ʔ 'corn roasted on open fire'

ʔojéɔʔtaʔ (identical with the preceding)

watéʔskɔ:tak 'it's been baked'

watéʔjɛ:ɔtak (identical with the preceding)

ʔä:hkwaʔ 'bread'

ká:hkɔ:tak 'baked bread'

ká:hkok 'boiled bread'

kakaehtɛ́htaʔ or kakaehtɛ́htɔh 'corn bread'

ka:hkwakí:ʔta:ʔ 'ghost bread,' literally 'fried bread'

kanɛɔthéʔtɔh 'early bread,' literally 'pounded corn'

ʔothéʔshäʔ 'flour'

ʔonɛ́ɔʔ ʔo:nɔʔ 'corn oil'

Beans

The generic word for 'bean' is ʔosáeʔtaʔ [o-si-dä—LHM]. Most or all belong to the genus *Phaseolus*, but they have not been further identified. Names for kinds of beans are:

ha:yok 'Roman or cockleberry bean' (RE)

teká:ka:ha:t, literally 'it lies with legs outspread'

ʔawέɔta:kɔh literally 'deep-colored flower' ('purple kidney'—ACP)

ʔosáeʔtakɛ:ɛt 'white bean'

ʔotikɔhsó:aʔ, literally 'their heads are on the end of a stick'

ʔóeäʔke:kha:ʔ 'cornstalk variety'

káiskɛʔse:ʔ 'sparrow'

tyothɔwɛtɔh 'hummingbird'

ʔotkówɔʔsa:aʔ 'string bean'

Other classifications of beans are:

yɔʔɛnothaʔ 'pole bean,' literally 'they set up a pole'
   (cf. yɔʔɛnotáhkwaʔ 'bean pole,' literally 'they use it for setting up a pole')

ʔonósäʔah 'soft or young beans'

Bean preparations are:

ʔosáeʔta:kiʔ 'bean soup'

ʔojískwaʔ 'mush,' made from beans as well as corn

Squash

The generic term for *Cucurbitaceae* is ʔo:nyóhsaʔ. The following kinds are distinguished:

ʔo:nyáʔsaʔ 'crookneck squash,' literally 'neck'

ʔo:nyóhsaʔɔ:weh 'scalloped squash,' literally 'native or Indian squash'

ʔoshéʔto:t 'Hubbard squash,' literally 'navel'

ʔoʔyáka:ɛt [o-gä-gä-ind—LHM (?)] 'gray squash' (LHM), literally 'anus'

ʔo:nyóskwä:eʔ 'cucumber'

ʔo:nyóhsowa:nɛh 'pumpkin,' literally 'big squash'

ʔo:nyóhsatkos 'watermelon' (*Citrullus vulgaris*), literally 'raw squash'

wa:ya:is 'muskmelon' (*Cucumis melo*), literally 'the fruit ripens'

Another related term is **ʔoʔóhsaʔ** 'vine.' Squash preparations are:

ka:nyóhsok 'boiled squash'
waté:nyɔhsɔ:tak 'baked squash'

Other Cultivated Plants

ʔoktéä ʔ 'carrot' (*Daucus carota*), 'beet' (*Beta vulgaris*), 'turnip' (*Brassica rapa*), literally 'root'
ʔonónɔʔta ʔ 'potato'
ʔoʔnóhsa ʔ 'onion' (*Allium sp.*)
ʔawɛtoʔké:a ʔ 'pea' (*Pisum sp.*)

Fruits

The generic term for fruit or berry is **ʔoji:ya ʔ** or, less commonly, **ʔo:ya ʔ**. Kinds of fruits are:

ʔo:ya:ji ʔ 'blueberry' ('huckleberry' — RE) (*Vaccinium sp.*), literally 'dark berry'
kɛhtáʔke:a ʔ 'high bush blueberry' (*Vaccinium sp.*)
nohkwakáiʔni ʔ 'low bush blueberry' (*Vaccinium sp.*)
(ʔo)jistɔtáʔshä ʔ 'strawberry' (*Fragaria sp.*) literally 'embers on it'
shésʔa:h 'small wild strawberry' (*Fragaria sp.*)
takwáʔtä:nɛ ʔ 'raspberry' (*Rubus sp.*)
thɔtaʔktɔ ʔ 'black raspberry' (*Rubus occidentalis*), literally 'bent stem'
ʔotkä:shä ʔ 'blackberry' (*Rubus sp.*)
ʔonɔ:shä ʔ 'thimbleberry' (*Rubus sp.*)
joʔä:ka ʔ wa:ya:s 'gooseberry' (*Ribes sp.*), literally 'raccoon eats the berries'
kaʔnéhsa ʔ 'nannyberry' (*Viburnum lentago*)
ʔosháista ʔ wa:ya:s 'partridgeberry' (*Mitchella repens*), literally 'snake eats the berries'
ʔe:i ʔ 'wild cherry' (*Prunus serotina*)
kanɔjóhkwanɛ ʔ 'fire cherry' (*Prunus pennsylvanica*)
teyakonyáʔthä:ʔs 'chokecherry' (*Prunus virginiana*), literally 'it chokes people'
kɛ́:eh 'plum' (*Prunus sp.*)
kanyaʔó:ya ʔ 'apple' (*Pyrus sp.*)
jóikto:wa ʔ 'wild crab apple,' literally 'great thorn'
káɛhtä:e ʔ 'peach' (*Prunus persica*), literally 'fuzz on it'

A fruit preparation is ꞏo:ya:kiꞏ 'berry water,' used for ceremonial purposes.

Nuts

The word for 'nut' is ꞏo:nyóꞏkwaꞏ. Kinds of nuts are:

jo:nyóꞏkwe:s 'butternut' (*Juglans cinerea*), literally 'long nut'

jo:nyóꞏkwa:k 'black walnut' (*Juglans nigra*), literally 'let it eat the nut'

ꞏonɔnoka:aꞏ, jistakέ:εꞏ, jokä:ka:s 'hickory' (*Carya ovata;* cf. p. 46)

ꞏo:nyóꞏkwajiwakεh 'bitter nut (hickory),' (*Carya cordiformis*)

ꞏo:nyéꞏstaꞏ 'chestnut' (*Castanea dentata*)

ꞏohsówiꞏshäꞏ 'hazelnut' (*Corylus sp.*)

ꞏoskέꞏεꞏ 'beechnut' (*Fagus grandifolia*)

ꞏoko:wäꞏ 'acorn' (*Quercus sp.*)

Other Plant Foods

ꞏo:nyókwiꞏsäꞏ 'grape' (*Vitis sp.*)

ꞏonɔ:skäꞏ 'milkweed'(*Asclepias sp.*)

ꞏotkóꞏtaꞏ 'sumac' (*Rhus sp.*)

Meat

The word for 'meat' is ꞏoꞏwá:ꞏ. Other terms are:

ꞏoꞏwá:se:ꞏ 'fresh meat'

ꞏoyéꞏkwä:ikɔh 'smoked (meat)'

ꞏojíkheꞏta:eꞏ 'salted (meat)'

ꞏɔhjíꞏä:ꞏ 'fried meat'

ꞏo:nɔꞏ 'fat, grease, lard'

Mammals

neokεꞏ 'deer' (*Odoeoileus virginianus*)

nyakwaiꞏ 'bear' (*Ursus americanus*)

nɔkanyáꞏkɔh 'beaver' (*Castor canadensis*), literally 'twig cutter'

se:nɔ:h 'skunk' (*Mephitis mephitis*)

théhto:ɔꞏ 'woodchuck' (*Marmota monax*)

jinotakaꞏ 'muskrat' (*Ondatra zibethica*)

jíoꞏta:kaꞏ 'mink' (*Mustela vison*)

joꞏä:kaꞏ 'raccoon' (*Procyon lotor*)

kwaꞏyɔ:ꞏ 'rabbit' (*Sylvilagus floridanus*)

thɔtayε:t 'hare' (*Lepus americanus*)

jokta:kɔꞏ 'gray or black squirrel' (*Sciurus carolinensis*)

joni:skyɔ:t 'red squirrel' (*Tamiasciurus hudsonicus*)
tha:wa:sɔ:t 'flying squirrel' (*Glaucomys sp.*)
kiskwi:s 'pig' (*Sus scrofa*)
tyó:skwaɔt 'cow' (*Bos taurus*)
ji:yäh 'dog' (*Canis familiaris*)

Birds

A 'bird' is called ji^ʔtɛ́ʔɔ:ʔ. Among the edible birds are:
so:wäk 'duck'
hɔka:k 'goose'
ʔoʔo:wa:ʔ 'owl'
johkwéʔeaniʔ 'ruffed grouse' (*Bonasa umbellus*)
kóhkwaiʔ 'quail'
nɔ́ʔjahkwɛʔ 'woodcock, snipe'
jako:ki:h 'blackbird'
tistis 'woodpecker'
tyó:yaik 'robin' (*Turdus migratorius*)
tekáyahtowanɛs 'meadowlark' (*Sturnella magna*), literally 'big thighs'
jä:hko:wa:ʔ 'pigeon,' literally 'great bread' (evidently because of the shape of its tail)
ʔoʔsó:ɔt 'turkey' (*Meleagris gallopavo*), literally 'pine on it'
takä:ʔɛ:ʔ 'chicken' (*Gallus gallus*)

Fish

The word for 'fish' is kɛjɔh. Among the edible fish are:
tya:wɛ:h 'trout'
kashéstaʔ 'sturgeon' (*Acipenser sp.*)
kaho:skwa:h 'dace'
jotä:tɔʔ 'bass'
joka:tkɛʔ 'pike' (*Esox sp.*)
katke:shäʔ (identical with the preceding), literally 'handle' (as an ax handle)
jikɔ́hse:s 'great northern pike' (*Esox lucius*), or 'pickerel' (*Esox sp.*), literally 'long face'
káisɛhtaʔ 'hammerhead' (*Hypentelium nigricans*)

Other Animal Foods

ʔokɔ:staʔ 'clam, oyster'
ʔonɔhsakéhteʔ 'snail,' literally 'house on its back'
skoʔäk 'frog'
haʔno:wa:h 'turtle'
kanyáhtɛ:h 'snapping turtle' (*Chelydra serpentina*)

ʔojíʔehtaʔ 'crayfish, crab, lobster'
kanɛ́:ithaʔ 'locust, cicada'
ʔoʔhóhsaʔ 'egg'
ʔonɔ́ʔkwaʔ 'milk'
ʔowi:sä? 'butter' (also 'ice')

Other Foods

ʔowä:nɔʔ 'maple sugar, sugar, candy'
kä:nɔ:nih 'honey'
ʔoshéstaʔ 'syrup, corn syrup'
ʔojíkheʔtaʔ 'salt'
teyósaeʔt '(black) pepper'
ʔonähsaʔ 'fungus'
tewátyɛʔkweokwas 'puffball' (*Calvatia gigantea*), literally
    'smoke scatters'
ʔatɛ́ɔno:shäʔ 'mushroom,' literally 'umbrella'

5. Names of People and Places

A. Races and Tribes

Indians are called ʔɔkwéʔɔ:weh, literally 'real, genuine, native
people.' A white man is ha:nyɔ́ʔɔh, in the plural hatí:nyɔʔɔh.
The Iroquois are hotínɔhsɔ:ni:h, literally 'house builders.'
Names for Iroquois tribes are:

(ʔo)nɔtowáʔka:ʔ 'Seneca,' literally 'people of the big hill'
kayókwe:onɔʔ 'Cayuga'
ʔonɔ́taʔke:ka:ʔ 'Onondaga,' literally 'people on the hill'
nɛ́yotka:ʔ 'Oneida,' literally 'people of the standing rock'
kanyɛ́ʔke:onɔʔ 'Mohawk,' literally 'people of the flint'
táske:owɛʔ 'Tuscarora'

B. Reservations

tyonɔ́hsate:kɛh 'Cornplanter,' literally 'burned house'
ʔohi:yoʔ 'Allegany,' literally 'beautiful river'
kaʔtä:kɛ́skɛ:ɔʔ 'Cattaraugus,' literally 'formerly the chimney
    (clay?) smelled'
tha:nɔwɔteʔ 'Tonawanda,' literally 'his rapids are there'
swe:kɛʔ 'Grand River (Six Nations),' also 'Canada'; swekéː:onɔʔ
    'person from Grand River or Canada'
taskéowɛʔkeh 'Tuscarora'
ʔonɔ́taʔkeh 'Onondaga,' literally 'on the hill'

kanɔktiyóʔkeh (identical with the preceding), literally 'at the good place'
kanyέʔkeh (any Mohawk reservation)

C. Longhouses

On the Allegany Reservation

tyo:nekano:h 'Coldspring,' literally 'cold water'
tetyóteha:ʔktɔ:h 'Horseshoe' (extinct), literally 'bent back upon itself, horseshoe curve'

On the Cattaraugus Reservation

tkanɔtase:ʔ 'Newtown,' literally 'new town'
ʔoʔsóäkɔ:h 'Pinewoods' (extinct), literally 'in the pines'
skɛhɔ:tih 'Indian Hill' (extinct), literally 'beyond the creek'
tɛ:nɔtyɛʔkwä:ʔhɔ:t 'Sandy's Road' (extinct), literally 'their smokes are joined together' (said to have been called this because it was an amalgamation of two even older longhouses)
taʔtewahkέɔtkeh 'Cayuga Street' (extinct), literally 'without eaves'

On the Tonawanda Reservation

kanɔtakɔ:h, literally 'in the town'
ʔoʔsóäkɔ:h 'Sand Hill' (extinct), literally 'in the pines'

D. Important Cities and Towns

tósyɔ:wɛ:h or tetyó:syo:kɛ:h 'Buffalo'
ska:néhtatih 'Albany,' literally 'beyond the plateau' (or 'pine')
tyo:ɔkot or heyó:ɔkɛh 'Akron, N. Y.'
jokɔwɔtih 'Gowanda,' literally 'beyond the ridge'
tyohátɛʔsyɔʔ or tyɔ:teokɛʔ 'Pittsburgh'
ka:nɔwɔkɔ:h 'Warren, Pa.,' literally 'in the rapids'
tkanɔtayέʔko:wa:h 'Philadelphia,' literally 'big town there'

E. Important Individuals

kayέthwahkeh 'Cornplanter,' literally 'where it is planted' (?)
shakóye:wa:thaʔ 'Red Jacket,' literally 'he makes them look for it in vain'
thέ:wɔ:nyaʔs 'Governor Blacksnake,' literally 'he breaks wire, nails'
kayáhsothaʔ 'Kyashota,' literally 'it stands up a cross'
shosheowa:ʔ [sose-ha'-wä—LHM] 'Great Burden Strap'

6. Supernatural Beings and Objects

The Supreme Being and his opposite number are referred to with the following words:

hotyɛ:nóʔktaʔɔh 'the Creator,' literally 'he has created it'; also hotyɛ:nóʔktaʔɔ hé tyɔheʔ 'he has created our lives'

haʔníkɔ:iyo:h (identical with the preceding), literally 'his mind is good'

hawɛni:yoʔ 'God' (the Christian term), literally 'his word is good' or possibly 'he is free'

haʔníkɔ:etkɛʔ 'the Devil,' literally 'his mind is evil'

shakoewáthaʔ (identical with the preceding), literally 'he punishes people'

haníshe:onɔʔ 'the Devil' (the Christian term), literally 'pit dweller'

Beings and objects frequently referred to in the calendrical ceremonies are:

ke:i niɛnɔti:h 'the Four Beings' ('Messengers, Angels')

hatiɔyáʔke:onɔʔ (identical with the preceding), literally 'sky dwellers'

ʔotáʔeoɔh (the mythical source of the wind), literally 'it's covered by a veil'

hatiwɛnotatyeʔs 'the Thunderers,' literally 'they are spreading the word'

hiʔnɔʔ [he'-no—LHM] 'the Thunderer'

Supernatural beings associated with the noncalendrical medicine ceremonies include:

jɔkã:ɔʔ or joʔkã:ɔʔ 'little people, pygmies, dwarfs, elves'

shakotyowéhko:wa:h (the false-face prototype), literally 'their great defender' (?)

ʔoshataʔké:aʔ 'Dew Eagle' (WNF), literally 'mist dweller'

Other mythological beings are:

hathoʔ 'Jack Frost' (RE), 'Frost God' (ACP)

hoskɛʔɛkéhtako:wa:h 'God of War' (ACP), literally 'great warrior'

jáɛnɔsko:wa:h 'Blue Lizard' (ACP)

jiskɛ:h 'skeleton, ghost'

jotéhkwatɔh 'Great Horned Serpent' (ACP)

káhkako:wa:h 'Giant Raven' (WNF)

kanɔ́ʔkwe:s 'Big Breast'

kasháistowanɛh 'Big Snake' ('Horned Snake'—ACP)

ká:syɔtye:tha? 'Fire Beast' (ACP), also 'lion'

kɛ:nɔ:skwa? 'Stone Giant,' literally 'it used to eat skin (or leather)'

nɔkanyá?kɔh 'White Beaver' (ACP), literally 'beaver'

nyá?kwaehe:h or nyá?kwaeheko:wa:h 'Great Bear' (Great Naked Bear'—ACP)

shakowe:nóa? 'Tide Spirit' (ACP), literally 'he ferries people'

shako?tatáhkwas 'He-Who-Eats-Inwards' (ACP), literally, 'he takes out people's feces'

shɔtowähko:wa:h 'Blue Panther' (ACP)

takwánɔ?ɛ:yɛt 'Wind Spirit' (ACP), 'Flying Head' (RE), literally 'hit us with a head!'

tá:tahwat or tá?tahkwat 'White Beaver' (ACP)

teotya?tyá?kɔh 'Divided Body (Hail Spirit)' (ACP), literally 'his body is cut in two'

tetyoswinéhtɔh 'Spring God' (ACP), literally 'it has thawed'

tewathyawɔ́:ɛ?s (?) 'Exploding Wren' (ACP)

tháyatkwa:i? (another mythical animal)

tó:nɔ?ka:es 'Horned Snake' (ACP), literally 'he has long horns'

?o?nɛ:yɔ:t 'Sharp-Legs' (ACP)

?o?nówatkɔ? 'Corn-Bug' (ACP), literally 'bug with evil power'

?o?nya:thɛ:h 'Little Dry Hand' (ACP), literally 'dry hand'

?ɔ́:i? (a mythical flying snake)

Power or strength, whether natural or supernatural, is ka?hásteshä?. Evil power is ?otkɔ?, and a witch is hotkɔ? if a man, kotkɔ? if a woman. kaháih, translated 'Will-of-the-Wisp' by ACP, refers to magical transformation, generally for an evil purpose.

Abbreviations

The following abbreviations were used in the glossary to identify terminology associated with a particular source:

ACP	Arthur C. Parker
FWW	Frederick W. Waugh
HCC	Harold C. Conklin and William C. Sturtevant
LHM	Lewis H. Morgan
ML	Marjorie Lismer
MRH	Mark R. Harrington
RE	Reservation English
WNF	William N. Fenton

Bibliography

A complete list of publications in which Seneca terms are included would occupy an unwarranted amount of space here; the reader is best referred to the Murdock bibliography cited below. The works which follow were found to be of particular usefulness in the preparation of the glossary.

Wallace L. Chafe

1960-61. "Seneca morphology." *International Journal of American Linguistics,* vols. 26-27.

Harold C. Conklin, & William C. Sturtevant

1953. "Seneca Indian singing tools at Coldspring longhouse." *Proceedings of the American Philosophical Society,* vol. 97, pp. 262-90.

William N. Fenton

1936. "An outline of Seneca ceremonies at Coldspring longhouse." *Yale University Publications in Anthropology,* No. 9. New Haven, Conn.

1941. "Masked medicine societies of the Iroquois." *The Smithsonian Report for 1940,* pp. 397-430. Washington, D. C.

1942. "Contacts between Iroquois herbalism and colonial medicine." *The Smithsonian Report for 1941,* pp. 503-26. Washington, D. C.

1950. "The roll call of the Iroquois chiefs." *Smithsonian Miscellaneous Collections,* vol. 111, No. 15. Washington, D. C.

1961. "Iroquoian culture history: a general evaluation." *Bureau of American Ethnology Bulletin 180,* pp. 253-77.

William N. Fenton, & Gertrude P. Kurath

1951. "The Feast of the Dead, or Ghost Dance at Six Nations Reserve, Canada." *Bureau of American Ethnology Bulletin 149,* pp. 139-65.

1953. "The Iroquois eagle dance: an offshoot of the calumet dance." *Bureau of American Ethnology Bulletin 156.*

Mark R. Harrington

1908. "Some Seneca corn-foods and their preparation." *American Anthropologist,* new series, vol. 10, pp. 575-90.

Gertrude P. Kurath

1951. "Local diversity in Iroquois music and dance." *Bureau of American Ethnology Bulletin 149,* pp. 109-37.

1952. "Matriarchal dances of the Iroquois." In Sol Tax, ed. *Indian Tribes of Aboriginal America,* vol. 3, pp. 123-30. Chicago, Ill.

Marjorie Lismer

1941. "Seneca splint basketry." *Indian Handicrafts,* No. 4. Washington, D. C.

Lewis H. Morgan

1871. "Systems of consanguinity and affinity of the human family." *Smithsonian Contributions to Knowledge,* vol. 17.

1901. *League of the Ho-dé-no-sau-nee or Iroquois.* Herbert M. Lloyd, *ed.* 2 vols. New York.

George P. Murdock

1960. *Ethnographic bibliography of North America,* pp. 234-46. New Haven, Conn.

Arthur C. Parker

1909. "Secret medicine societies of the Seneca." *American Anthropologist,* new series, vol. 2, pp. 161-85.

1909. "Snow-snake as played by the Seneca-Iroquois." *American Anthropologist,* new series, vol. 2, pp. 250-56.

1910. "Iroquois uses of maize and other food plants." *New York State Museum Bulletin 144.* Albany.

1913. "The code of Handsome Lake, the Seneca prophet." *New York State Museum Bulletin 163.* Albany.

1916. "The Constitution of the Five Nations." *New York State Museum Bulletin 184.* Albany.

1923. "Seneca myths and folk tales." *Publications of the Buffalo Historical Society,* vol. 27. Buffalo.

Frederick W. Waugh

1916. "Iroquois foods and food preparation." *Canada Department of Mines, Geological Survey, Memoir 86.* Ottawa, Canada.

Index

CPSIA information can be obtained
at www.ICGtesting.com
Printed in the USA
BVOW10s0817190717
489685BV00007B/134/P